I Can't Be
an Addict—I'm
a Christian

Also by Melinda Fish

Adult Children and the Almighty: Recovering from the
  Wounds of a Dysfunctional Home
Restoring the Wounded Woman: Recovering from Heart-
  ache and Discouragement
I'm So Tired of Acting Spiritual: Peeling Back the Mask
The River Is Here: Receiving and Sustaining the Blessing
  of Revival

I Can't Be
an Addict—I'm
a Christian

Melinda Fish

SPIRE

© 1990 by Melinda Fish

Published by Fleming H. Revell
a division of Baker Book House Company
P.O. Box 6287, Grand Rapids, MI 49516-6287

Spire edition published 1999

Previously published under the title *When Addiction Comes to Church: Helping Yourself and Others Move into Recovery*

Printed in the United States of America

ISBN 0-7394-0412-1

For current information about all releases from Baker Book House, visit our web site:
http://www.bakerbooks.com

To

Edward Brown

In Grateful Appreciation

The author would like to gratefully acknowledge the helpful support of the following people:

My husband, Bill, and my children, Sarah and Bill, for sacrificing themselves to help me and to see this book come about

My mother, Merle Wilson, for giving me the vision as a child to write and teaching me how

My extended family—the Fishes, the Weirs and the Wilsons —for supporting me emotionally

'The recovering addicts and ACOAs and the other brothers and sisters in Christ at Church of the Risen Saviour, Trafford, Pennsylvania, whose love and prayers have made the book possible

The recovering addicts who shared their painful experiences with me in the hope that others may be free

Leonard and Sandra LeSourd who inspired me to write this book and who unselfishly gave of their knowledge and skills to help me

Pastor and Mrs. A.J. Rowden, the Rev. Roberta Crane, the Rev. Earl and Vera Roundtree and the other friends of Evangelistic Center Church, Kansas City, Missouri, who prayed for me as I wrote

Buddy and Mary Ann Brown who prayed for me and shared their wisdom

The Rev. Jim and Joyce Hart for their prayers and advice

The Rev. and Mrs. Elliott Tepper, missionaries in Madrid, Spain, among the drug addicts and alcoholics, for their loving prayers and for the experiences they have shared to help addicts recover

Ann McKay, Montreat, North Carolina, for sharing her experience in the Mexico City earthquake

Chris Tabb whose artwork graces the pages of chapter 8.

The following other professionals for their expert advice and counsel:

Dr. Ronald L. Rogers, M.D., Lake Jackson, Texas

Louis A. LaGatta, executive director of Hope Counseling Services, New Castle, Pennsylvania

Dr. John D. Kristofic, M.D., Penn Hills, Pennsylvania

Dr. Sue Barrick Miller, psychologist, Fields-Miller Associates, Monroeville, Pennsylvania

Dr. Ruth Seilhamer, psychologist, Fields-Miller Associates, Monroeville, Pennsylvania

The Rev. Dr. Bob Seilhamer, psychotherapist and pastor of St. Mark's Lutheran Church, Trafford, Pennsylvania

Glenda Moser, M.A., certified in addiction counseling

Inspector Dave Liebrum, Pennsylvania State Police, Beaver County

Jane Campbell, John Sherrill and Ann McMath of Chosen Books for tireless editing

David Hazard, writer and friend, for advice and counsel.

Contents

Contents

I Can't Be
an Addict—I'm
a Christian

1
Addiction: The Root of So Much Misery

Jan Stewart* is only 25 years old. When she was twenty she left a life of drugs and alcohol, to the delight of her parents and friends who were praying for her, and turned full swing to Jesus Christ. From then on, Jan gave it her all to make up for lost time spiritually. She never missed a service and attended every church work day and social event. Not content only to hear the Word preached to her, Jan took several courses at a local Bible college. She donated her time to helping in the church office, and her gentle, quiet presence made her loved and appreciated by the pastor and other leaders of the church. In those five years, Jan changed from a caterpillar to a butterfly, shedding a drab cocoon and blossoming into an attractive, capable woman. She landed a job at a downtown company where she earned promotions and plaques of merit.

---

* Throughout this book where confidential experiences are related, fictitious identifications are used, although the essentials of each story are true.

A few months ago, however, Jan's countenance began to change. A look of sullen sadness slowly enveloped her face as she plunged into what seemed like a period of depression. She stopped talking to her Christian friends but continued attending services. When her pastor's wife expressed her concern, she was not prepared for Jan's confession. No one ever would have guessed that during those several months, Jan was going every night to the bar near the bus stop downtown and gulping down alcohol. Try as she would, she could not stop herself until she satisfied a persistent drive to drink.

Prayer was not helping her, nor was increased Bible reading. Swallowed up by guilt and remorse, Jan was on the verge of leaving the church. "How could anyone who claims to love Jesus Christ do such a thing?" she had asked herself a thousand times. Her job performance was deteriorating as piles of work were left unfinished on her desk each evening. She was also suffering mild lapses of memory and feared she would be fired unless she could get control of herself. Life would be simpler, she thought, if she could just run away.

Frank is the pastor of a church of nearly two hundred members on the West Coast. Rescued from the streets of metropolitan Los Angeles by a street ministry team reaching drug addicts and alcoholics, Pastor Frank has been drug-clean and alcohol-free for nearly twenty years since his salvation experience. As pastor of his nondenominational, charismatic congregation, Frank rules with a loving but firm hand. Quick to correct and discipline, he wants to rescue every sheep from falling into the pit from which he barely escaped.

Several years after coming to Christ and sensing the call to the ministry, Frank met and married Sylvia, the daughter of a wealthy, white-collar alcoholic. With a marriage made in heaven, Frank and Sylvia minister at a pace that would drive less resilient men and women into an early grave. The parents of two teenage children who join with them in family ministry, Frank and Sylvia seem to have every waking moment consumed with feverish "spiritual" activity. Frank preaches a lot about excellence and "going out to your limits in God."

The staff runs to keep up with Frank's expansive, expensive dreams. Finances are never a problem for Frank's faith as he borrows on his personal credit line to purchase state-of-the-art equipment and furnishings for his church. The church debts are so far out of the financial reach of the current membership size that it will be years before they can be paid. In his early fifties, Frank has suffered for several years with heart disease but refuses to control his weight, which now balloons at just over three hundred pounds. His last trip to the doctor revealed coronary bypass surgery looming larger than life on the horizon.

With all the warning signs, it seems Frank would slow down, but he doesn't. Driven by a desire to excel, Frank has not stopped long enough to examine why he is so driven. Although he desires earnestly to see his church grow, he experiences massive turnover because his congregation is full of people just like him who cannot stop *doing* long enough to build vital human relationships, and others who are tired of being run over roughshod by Frank's dogmatic preaching, frantic pace and domineering approach to pastoring.

Ironically, the same problem is at the root of the misery in both Jan Stewart's and Pastor Frank's lives. Both Jan and Frank are undiagnosed, untreated addicts. One sits in the pew and the other stands behind the pulpit, and both desperately need help from God, help from the church and help from trained professionals.

Addiction Often Undiagnosed

Addiction is no longer a term linked only to drugs and alcohol. It also encompasses a gamut of substance addictions including chocolate, sweets, nicotine and caffeine. Recently the term has been used to describe the bondage that chains its victims to behaviors that can become compulsive—such as gambling, shopping, sex, exercise, TV-watching and work.

Addiction is a life-controlling process that leads its victims on a downward spiral toward destruction and death. These addictions are usually undetected and almost always unconfronted by friends and loved ones, who are often victims themselves.

Millions of dollars were spent last year treating addictions. In 1986, 1.5 million Americans received treatment for alcoholism in treatment centers, and in 1985, the worldwide Alcoholics Anonymous membership soared to more than 1,125,000, according to Norman Denzin in *Treating Alcoholism: An Alcoholics Anonymous Approach*. Weight-loss clinics are springing up in every city and small town and fad diets continue to make the bestseller lists. Hardly a week goes by that some TV talk show is not devoted to addiction treatment. In the past three years, sports heroes and televangelists have fallen from honor to reproach because of addiction. Both political parties during the 1988 presidential campaign included planks in their platforms outlining plans to fight the war on drugs. People from every stratum of society from skid row to the White House are looking for an answer to the addiction plague.

I was brought up in a Christian home where drinking alcohol is against family tradition. My great-grandfather was a medical doctor and an alcoholic. But in a day when there was no

Alcoholics Anonymous or co-dependency support groups, my shouting Methodist great-grandmother defied the mores of the nineteenth century and left him, taking her five children, their belongings and a picture of John Wesley.

Her courageous decision to live in an alcohol-free environment has resulted in three succeeding generations without active alcoholism. Any tendencies in family members toward that socially acceptable drug have been defused by saying no. And yet most of the misery in my life has been rooted, indirectly, in alcohol and drugs.

For thirteen years I have co-pastored alongside my husband, Bill, in a church where an astonishing ninety percent of the members are adult children of alcoholics (ACOAs). Many are recovering addicts. As Bill and I share the liberating Gospel of Jesus Christ with such a congregation we have experienced much joy—and pain.

Both are included in the pages of this book as I look over what we are learning. But I do not write only from other people's experiences. I have battled food addiction myself and I will be talking about that as well in this discussion of Christians and addiction.

I have also interviewed pastors, counselors and lay leaders, many of whom are discouraged at the increasing drop-out rate in the Church, a figure affected drastically by the failure of the Church to diagnose and treat addiction. Having tried many approaches and seen what works and what doesn't, and having searched the Bible for answers, I am relieved to tell you that there is hope—hope in Jesus Christ for the addict, Christian or otherwise.

But before we continue, my teacher's instincts tell me it's time for a "pop quiz." Please take a pencil in hand and answer *true* or *false* to each of the following 22 questions.

_____ 1. *Addiction* is a twentieth-century concept not found in the Bible.

_____ 2. Addiction is more likely to happen to non-Christians than to Christians.

_____ 3. Once a person becomes a Spirit-filled Christian, he is automatically delivered from drugs and alcohol and should never again refer to himself as an "addict."

_____ 4. The term *addiction* is limited to the use of substances taken into the body.

_____ 5. All addicts choose to continue using their addictive substances.

_____ 6. Addictions are little more than moral weaknesses.

_____ 7. If a person has enough willpower, he can overcome any addiction, because addiction is controllable through will power alone.

_____ 8. Addiction scars the body only—not the mind or the spirit.

_____ 9. All addictions left unchecked lead to some sort of death.

_____10. It is possible to be addicted to only one or two substances at a time.

_____11. Once a person stops using an addictive substance, he can consider himself "cured" of that particular addiction.

_____12. There is no scientific evidence to support the belief that the tendency toward addiction is transmitted from generation to generation.

_____13. When a church member goes back to taking alcohol or drugs, it is a symptom of a "spiritual problem" only.

_____14. Deliverance from addiction is usually instantaneous.

_____15. Families and friends of addicts should, in love, help cover the addict's problem until he can get control of himself.

_____16. The Bible says that everything is good—but in moderation.

_____17. Addiction affects only the addict himself and is, therefore, a personal problem and no one else's business.

_____18. Addicts are most commonly found in lower socio-economic classes.

_____19. Addictions are better left alone because they are too painful to face directly, and they will likely disappear on their own.

_____20. A person truly cured of addiction can once again use the addictive substance moderately without fear of becoming re-addicted.

_____21. In order to be considered an "addict," a person has to overindulge himself daily.

_____22. An addiction is only a physical disease. It doesn't involve sin on any level.

The answers to all the questions spell *controversy*, but only number nine is true. If this leaves you with questions about yourself or a loved one, I hope you will read on. This book will provide the answers you desperately need. What is the difference between a habit and an addiction? Does watching a favorite TV program at the same time every week constitute addiction? Is addiction a sin or a disease? What causes a person to become addicted? How can friends and family members help? How much should you take from an addict before you confront? What are the symptoms of addictive behavior?

We will look at case studies of Christians and see why conversion alone does not necessarily overcome a chemical dependency. We will also meet other brothers and sisters in Christ who are battling one or more process addictions—and see how freedom is found. Once called "bad habits," the range of process addictions, which includes such things as workaholism, sex addiction, shopaholism and gambling, does not involve the ingestion of substances, but rather addictive actions that catch the victim in a compulsive, predictable cycle and fling him toward destruction.

I Can't Be an Addict—I'm a Christian not only explores the problem, but contains scriptural answers that do not cloud the issue with more denial. It shows the keys in God's Word that can bring the addict out of bondage, through the wilderness of emotional healing and into the promised land of "normalcy" by restoring the soul and renewing the mind. We will learn to look more closely at the emotional wounds that control compulsive behaviors, actions that vie for the place of lordship that belongs only to Jesus Christ. This is not a "quick-fix" approach, but a solid, gradual cure that works.

It may have been a little uncomfortable to pick up a book entitled *I Can't Be an Addict—I'm a Christian*. It could mean that either you or someone you dearly love is undoubtedly caught in the quagmire of shame surrounding an area of life that has gone out of control. Although the word *addict* may have seemed a little strong, you drew a breath and reached out for the book anyway, half hoping it would help confirm that your worst fear—the fear of true addition—was groundless. Or perhaps you already know about addiction's cruel trap and are desperately seeking a way out. In your own private way, reaching for this book was like reaching out to God. Let me assure you that God looked behind your fears and read into the simple act a brave cry for help. What you did, my friend, took "guts," and whether you know it or not, it was your first small step toward freedom.

This book is about to explode some of the devil's most popular myths about addiction. Believing these myths has kept countless millions in bondage. In this book I am out to change your mind and heart with the truth about addiction and provide you with the resources you need to conquer this fatal foe.

2
What Is
Addiction?

What is an addict? On August 10, 1989, NBC aired a documentary entitled "Fatal Addictions," revealing to the prime-time American public what those observing the trend have feared: Addiction is fast becoming America's number-one social ill. No longer is the term *addiction* applied only to the alcoholic or the drug addict. The term is now being applied to a wide range of compulsive behaviors that chain their victims to various substances and processes.

Like life-sucking tentacles, the manifestations of addiction wrap themselves around a victim—whom we will call an addict—giving his various natural appetites an artificial life of their own, while simultaneously short-circuiting their ability to function normally. It is possible for someone to become addicted to food, spending, sex, soap operas, physical exercise, work, gambling, nicotine, caffeine, a host of chemicals and prescription drugs, an unhealthy relationship or any initially pleasurable activity. As a victim of those invisible tentacles, the addict begins to feel the devastating effects spiritually, emotionally and physically. Without help he will be physically and morally degraded, reduced to a devastated shadow of what he could have been. As addiction progresses further, he will lose self-respect and will often lose the relationships of those closest to him who are left to stand by helplessly while a force they are unable to see slowly claims from the addict the very best life has to offer him.

Ironically, the addiction itself remains covert and unidentified. In most cases its presence is even denied or misdiagnosed, facilitating its clandestine operation. The victims most vulnerable are those in need. In the beginning they seek a pleasurable substance or pastime to ease pain, bring a sense of relief to boredom or fill a void.

It is wrong to assume that anyone ever sets out to become an addict; rather he desires only to fill a natural need. But regardless of how long it takes, addiction lies in wait, seldom missing its chance to devour its prey.

In order to clarify the nature of this force in our own lives and the lives of those we love, it will be necessary to define addiction, and for that we must turn to several sources for help.

What Doctors Say About Addiction

Medical professionals concur that addiction begins when the line separating it from abuse is crossed. The abuser is in control, the true addict is not. The addict may believe, in a time of abstinence, that he is in control, but eventually he will discover that days, weeks, months or even years apart from it make little difference: He snaps back as though he were attached to it with a piece of elastic. No matter how far away he seems to get, he will one day collide with his addiction again.

Dr. Bernard Green, a nutritionist and author of *Getting Over Getting High*, defines *substance addiction* as "the experience of being unable to immediately and permanently stop the use of a drug without suffering some degree of discomfort." This loss of control is the crux of the old Chinese proverb often quoted by members of Alcoholics Anonymous: "The man takes a drink, then the drink takes a drink, then the drink takes the man." Loss of control appears in everyone's definition of addiction. Sometimes quickly, sometimes gradually, but always eventually, the substance or process once sought to fill the emotional void and bring pleasure becomes the slave-driver. It demands repetitive use and threatens the victim with painful (and sometimes, as in the case of alcohol and hard drugs, fatal) withdrawals.

All substance and process addictions stimulate the portion of the brain known as the "pleasure center." (I wonder if this isn't part of what is included when the apostle Paul wrote, "In the last days . . . men will be . . . lovers of pleasure rather than lovers of God," 2 Timothy 3:1,2,4.) Stimulation of this center causes the receptors on the neurotransmitters of brain cells to multiply. When the addictive substance wears off, the newly created receptors begin to scream for stimulation. As the number of receptors multiplies with each use, more of the addictive substance is needed to produce the same degree of stimulation. This physiological phenomenon is responsible for the appearance of craving, which manifests in various forms ranging from violent physical symptoms such as nausea, D.T.s (delirium tremens), extreme anxiety and irritability, to something as seemingly mild as a repetitive thought that graduates to an obsession. The reason the pleasure center develops a craving for a certain form of stimulation is also beginning to be discovered.

Let's look at the phenomenon more closely. In *Growing Up Addicted*, Stephen Arterburn explains the brain's discerning taste for a particular form of stimulation. An alcoholic, for example, will crave alcohol rather than some other equally addictive chemical. He describes the process by which alcohol affects each person individually as *adaptation*, the ability of the brain to learn to function smoothly under the influence of the drug. As alcohol enters the body of the potential alcoholic, it is metabolized in a manner different from the way the non-alcoholic metabolizes it. The cells begin to alter the way they normally function in order to accommodate the use of alcohol. The body then begins to function smoothly only when the alcohol (or drug of choice) is in the bloodstream "nourishing" the cells of the body. Whenever it is not present in the body's system, "normal" begins to feel abnormal and eventually painful. It is then that the alcoholic begins to manifest, physically, the destructive disease phase. As toxins permeate the liver and other organ tissues, other diseases develop, such as cirrhosis, pancreatitis and some forms of arthritis.

Drug addiction produces similar effects and can lead to the contracting of secondary diseases. As calcium levels drop, drug addicts often lose their teeth. Infections begin to develop, some of which are related to careless usage. AIDS and endocarditis are rampant among communities of drug addicts. Elliott Tepper, WEC missionary and founder of Centro Betel, a ministry to drug addicts in Madrid, Spain, expects to lose most of his addicts to fatal diseases triggered by addiction in the next five years. "If the statistics have even a small measure of truth in them," he writes, "most of our people are not far from eternity."

But, as I have said, alcohol and drugs are not the only fatal addictions. Diane Fassel and Anne Wilson Schaef define addiction in their book *The Addictive Organization* this way: "If there is something we are not willing to give up in order to make our lives fuller and healthier, it probably can be classified as an addiction." Food addiction claims many more lives as victims eat themselves to death, going on binges with foods that produce toxic effects and contribute to the development of high cholesterol, high blood pressure, heart disease, strokes and some forms of cancer, as well as diabetes and aggravation of a large number of other ailments. As we will see in a later chapter, it is one of the most common and socially acceptable addictions in the Christian community.

Dan was the husband of a Christian woman and the father of two daughters whom he adored. He was employed at a chemical plant near the Texas Gulf Coast and was the treasurer of his Sunday school class at the Baptist church he attended faithfully every Sunday. The medical community was just beginning to discover the effects of high cholesterol on heart disease when Dan learned in his early forties that he was developing heart disease himself.

In spite of the instructions of his doctor, Dan could not resist filling his lunch pail with pimiento cheese, peanut-butter-and-banana sandwiches, chips and treats processed with saturated fat. His wife tried to get him to eat low-sodium meals and to forego his trips to Bo's Barbecue Stand. But Dan argued that eating was one of the few pleasures of life.

Several times over a period of fifteen years Dan collapsed with a fibrillating heart and had to be taken to the emergency room. Medication brought it under control until one October day when he suffered a massive heart attack. For several days

Dan lay near death as his wife and daughters alternately held his hand and wept in the hospital chapel. Dan survived, miraculously, but as he lay in bed he was already chuckling about his next trip to Bo's Barbecue. But Dan never left the hospital. He died suddenly one morning, the victim of another heart attack. He was 58 years old, and somehow I haven't quite gotten over it. He was my father. And as we watched, his addiction silently and slowly took its fatal toll.

Substance addictions are understood more easily in the light of the physical damage they cause, but what about process addictions? The term means becoming addicted to a pattern of behavior. Compulsive shopping, exercising, TV-watching can all be process addictions. The key words are *endorphin* and *dopamine*, neurotransmitters secreted by the body. These secretions are similar in molecular structure to morphine. The neurotransmitters stimulate the pleasure center, the area of the limbic system located deep within the temporal lobe of the brain. According to *The Encyclopedia of Psychoactive Drugs*, it is becoming apparent that both pleasurable or stressful experiences trigger the release of neurotransmitters in the body, directly affecting behavior and producing a "high" similar to the highs experienced with substance addictions.

The "endorphin high" is believed to be responsible for the "rush" that accompanies the anorexic's slow starvation. To keep itself going in the face of reduced nourishment, the body's pituitary gland begins to secrete endorphins, which provide a natural but substitutional charge replacing the energy it once received from food. It is the same sort of high experienced after a hard workout. Anorexics, like bulimics who binge on food, often purge themselves through pro-

27

longed exercise or the use of laxatives or self-induced vomiting. These activities generate the increased release of endorphins and adrenalin into the bloodstream. The compulsive-addictive nature of these diseases is now believed to be rooted in the rush obtained through the endorphin-induced high.

The same high is believed to be linked to other process addictions. Whether it involves the shopaholic who "turns on" at the smell of the perfume counter at the mall; the sexaholic who seeks relief in the sex act several times a day, eventually turning to pornography, sexual abuse in the marriage relationship, prostitution and sex offenses; the compulsive gambler whose rush comes from placing more and more bets; or the sportsaholic who gets high on the "thrill of victory and the agony of defeat," in its effect on relationships, process addiction is as destructive as substance addiction.

Addiction, to the medical profession, is not only a physical disease, but also an emotional one brought on by the brain's repeated exposure to the stimulation of its pleasure center through the use of an addictive substance or process. An addiction produces predictable symptoms, and it progresses in identifiable stages producing gradual degeneration in the body and distorting the ability of the emotions and reasoning powers to function normally. Once a "friend," the addiction now turns on its victim, unleashing its full fury. It produces moral degeneration, forcing the victim to compromise his own principles and violate reason in exchange for the high. Perhaps this more than any other factor in addiction causes it to be a source of shame not only to those around the addict, but to the addict himself.

Whereas the addict may once have been an agreeable, pleasant person, substance addiction and even some process addictions transform him into an ill-tempered stranger. His emotions become raw, often causing him to erupt like a volcano. Stubbornness and manipulation develop toward any suggestion that his behavior may need to change. Often his moods swing quickly from periods of happiness and elation to the pits of depression. As the disorder progresses, he becomes more secretive about his use of the addictive substance or involvement in the addictive process. Such was the case with a couple my husband and I knew who attended a neighboring church and whom I shall call Clyde and Fay James.

Clyde and Fay caused the heads of their pastors to shake in disbelief. For the third time in four years of professed Christianity, they left their church in a huff and were not seen for six months. Clyde and Fay had been "bikers" before leaving their wolf-pack existence to come to Jesus Christ. On a bet, they had wandered into a Christian rock concert and wound up being born again and receiving the Holy Spirit. The charismatic church they attended was thrilled to see Clyde and Fay drop their association with their motorcycle gang and begin to make changes in their lives. Like the ghoulish tattoos on Clyde's arms, though, there were certain things that never changed. Clyde and Fay persisted in wearing their "leathers" and roaring up to the services on Clyde's Harley, Fay's hair stringing in the wind as Clyde gave one final rev of the engine before turning it off. Their pastors sometimes wondered if their pasts had truly been erased after all. Periods of anxiety and irritability would strike Clyde, usually in the spring, and he would fly off the handle at the slightest provocation. Fay would follow him in his rebellious stew, which sometimes lasted for several weeks but always culminated in his roaring out of town on his bike, Fay holding onto his waist.

When Clyde and Fay did return, they blamed the church. The other members of the congregation walked on eggshells around Clyde because he was so unpredictable. Fay would try to be the peacemaker, but eventually she threw up her hands and yielded to his hot-tempered impulses.

But no one suspected that the real reason for their backsliding was Clyde's insatiable desire for a "fix." He simply had not been delivered at all.

Attempts to control an addiction through willpower almost always fail, plunging the addict into despair. These attempts to control the addiction only cause it to erupt in some other form of equally addictive behavior. Substitute addictions and "highs" replace the original addiction and present the appearance both to the addict and those around him that the addiction has been conquered.

Frank, the compulsive pastor in the first chapter, seems to those not knowledgeable about addiction to have been "delivered" from drugs and alcohol. Rather than face the addiction on the physical, emotional and spiritual levels, however, he has swallowed his addiction and turned to workaholism, food and compulsive spending to satisfy his need for a high.

While medical definitions are vital to our study of addiction, the question Christians often ask is, "What does the Bible have to say about addiction?"

Does the Bible Mention Addiction?

Since the Fall in the Garden of Eden, man has been unusually capable of getting into trouble with his human needs. After all, Eve got into trouble at the "grocery store." While looking for something to eat she came upon the tree God had declared off-limits. She lingered beneath its fruit-laden branches; it seemed such a shame to waste it all. Her mouth began to water. Surely God had created it for a reason. Didn't He give "us richly all things to enjoy" (1 Timothy 6:17, KJV)? Before Eve could think further, the serpent offered her just one tasty bite. Rationalizing away the instruction of the Lord God, she drew a breath and sank her teeth into the fruit's savory flesh. Still not recognizing the eternal implications of her action, she turned to her husband who was lingering a short distance away and offered him a bite. Adam, too, chose the succulent morsel. I doubt it was a very big bite and for a while it seemed not to matter—until they heard the sound of their Divine Companion striding to meet them.

What had actually happened to Adam and Eve? Their action hardly seems wicked to a world where right and wrong are judged on the basis of harm to others rather than hurt to God. But their God-created appetite sought satisfaction in the forbidden.

Since that moment, man has become susceptible to addiction.

The Garden of Eden story is not the only clue the Bible gives us to addiction. King Solomon, the Old Testament's wisest man, made frequent observations of drunkards and gluttons and recorded these observations in Scripture. What he wrote in Proverbs 23:30–35 describes the addiction process three thousand years before any of today's counselors ever saw their first addict. "Do not look on the wine when it is red," he wrote, "when it sparkles in the cup, when it goes down smoothly; at the last it bites like a serpent, and stings like a viper." This personification of the taste and effect of alcohol is loaded with revelation. Every addiction begins as an innocent quest for relief—"it goes down smoothly"—but like the sting of the viper, all unchecked addictions lead to death Whether it is physical death (alcoholism is the number-three killer in the United States, according to the National Institute on Alcohol Abuse and Alcoholism) or the death of a marriage because of sexual abuse or compulsive gambling, all addictions destroy lives.

Addiction was no stranger to the apostle Paul. In his writings to two of the early churches, he specifically prohibited the appointment of leaders who were addicts. The two Greek words he chose in speaking about the malady give clues to a biblical definition of addiction. To Timothy and Titus, Paul used the word *paroinos* when referring to those specifically addicted to wine. It actually means "beside wine," conjuring a picture of one always found near the bottle. In writing to Timothy in another place, Paul chose the word *prosecho* which means "to turn to." An addict, in the biblical sense, is one who turns to a substance or process in time of need.

The clearest picture in the Word of God illustrating the powerful bondage of addiction and the strength of God to break it is the story of the Hebrews' escape from slavery in the land of Egypt. It is the story of a loving God eager to come down and deliver His people from the hands of a cruel master. It reveals the compassionate heart of God in reaching down with a power greater than their chains and leading them step-by-step from the desert of Egypt to the Promised Land of Canaan. It is the closest parallel in the Bible to the journey of the addict and provides a perfect model for physical, emotional and spiritual healing. It is from this story that our prescription for healing will be drawn and applied to each phase of the addiction process and recovery. More than the story of a nation, Exodus foreshadows the delivering, healing power of Jesus Christ. In it lie God's secrets to overcoming the power of addiction's cruel bondage in any life. Now that we have examined what addiction is, let's look at how it develops. What causes a person to fall into the trap?

3
The Addictive Environment

"Woe to the rebellious children," declares the Lord, "who proceed down to Egypt, without consulting Me, to take refuge in the safety of Pharaoh, and to seek shelter in the shadow of Egypt! Therefore the safety of Pharaoh will be your shame, and the shelter in the shadow of Egypt, your humiliation." Isaiah 30:1–3

The caravan bearing Jacob, his sons and their families crossed the border into Egypt, entering a society that promised them more than something just to fill their hungry stomachs. The camels swayed under the weight of their possessions and the precious cargo of their children as their sweat evaporated quickly in the arid calm. The smallest puff of breeze carried the breath of spices and the mouth-watering scent of the stewing pots of meat in thousands of Egyptian homes. Palm trees rose like towering spindles out of the desert floor, their tops bursting into tufts of verdant fronds that veiled clusters of ripened dates. And there was the ever-present Nile, sacred river of the Egyptians, gently coursing its way from snow-capped mountains deep within the continent through thousands of miles of desert plain and into the waiting tributaries of the rich Nile delta. Upon arrival, they were greeted, as Joseph's kinsmen, with the accolades afforded only kings, and they relished the thought that this exotic and powerful land lay at their feet.

Egypt made a place for them, secure at her ever-flowing breast, and there they rested. Gone were the struggles of Canaan; the parched fields and empty wells were like the faded history of another people's past. The joy of reunion with Joseph, their pride in all he had overcome and the knowledge that they were saved at last gently lulled them to sleep and wiped away their tears. It was like a dream that had come to pass, and before them was set new hope—the opportunity to pursue life, freedom and happiness.

But four hundred years later, the ever-flowing breast had ceased to give its milk. The days dawned hot and dry over the sun-parched land of Egypt. The muddy brickpits lay waiting, watered with the wheels turned by thousands of Israelite feet drawing the Nile's still-sacred waters into the slave-dug trenches. The pungent odor of clay mud and cattle dung drew large, stinging flies to the whip-lashed backs of the slaves as they trudged the miles. Before dawn every Hebrew man, woman and child of age had been up laboring at the tedious task of preparing bricks, the building blocks of Pharaoh's grandiose dreams, the storage cities of Pithom and Ramses. The fields they passed were dotted with figures bent in harvesting straw, a necessary ingredient in brickmaking.

Nothing distinguished one day from any other day over the past several hundred years. Goshen, once a resort-like state for the kinsmen of Joseph, the hero of two countries, had become the ghetto of slaves. In the hundreds of years since Joseph had died, the Hebrews had been living a hellish nightmare. The place they had sought for refuge in a time of famine had filled their bellies, but in so doing, they had allowed it to capture their souls. One by one, the Egyptians had removed their rights, their properties, their possessions and their children until they were manipulated into serving the ruling class. Hardly a Hebrew lived whose back had not felt the whip's stinging lash, the gut-wrenching sorrow of seeing his children snatched away and sent to another field of labor and the humiliation of serving an idolatrous people who worshiped animals and despised the God of their fathers. For every morsel of food, they paid years of hard labor, poverty and disease.

By this time no one could remember what life had been like before the new order. Only stories were left of the glories of Joseph's prophetic powers that stole the Egyptian Pharaoh's heart and the lavish treatment the first Hebrew settlers had received upon their arrival in this once-exotic land. How the dream had turned into grief was all they knew now. Given the chance to live it again, would they have chosen Egypt or waited out the drought in Canaan?

Slavery to Egypt left scars on the Hebrews and their children. Just so, the society of our day is deeply scarred by the effects of its own form of slavery, a slavery to substances and processes. Our society is the first of three principal "institutions" that contribute to the development and maintenance of an atmosphere in which addiction festers.

The Addictive Society

We, like the ancient Egyptians, are a society adept at substituting a quick fix for the stress of living. We don't really know how to bear up gracefully in time of need because the societal message is that we need never suffer. There's always a McDonald's around the corner, a mall a mile away and a bar across the street. Every headache gets a pill or a cup of coffee and every lack is filled in two seconds.

We are a nation divided into three social classes: the wealthy who have others work for them while they concentrate on making more money, the middle working class of people who work for the wealthy and try to become wealthy, and the poor who live on welfare and only dream of wealth. The struggle to stay on top financially has become the nation's central pursuit. More money means more opportunities for pleasure and fewer interruptions in chasing the American dream, a dream in which "the pursuit of happiness" has been condensed into "more money." The lure of the "good life" is played out before our lusting eyes as television advertisers set the feverish pace of the addictive society's race for more.

But our greed is only a symptom of deeper hurts. We are a society filled with pain. Regardless of social class, every person must face the eventual possibility of shattered relationships. Almost fifty percent of marriages are ending in divorce. When friendships become uncomfortable, we simply discard them like the sandwich containers at Burger King.

All this emotional pain stems from the natural hunger of each man's soul for love and affection, meaningful communication, a sense of self-worth and the security of stable relationships.

The principal characteristic of the addictive society, the breeding ground for addiction, is the shattered dream. The addictive society dreams an unrealistic dream, encouraging a distorted picture of what real life is all about. But behind both the facade of gracious living and the wall of the ghetto is the same sad, lonely face of man separated from God and the others he dearly loves.

The Hurting Home

The home, the second institution contributing to the development of addiction, is one place where the shattered dream manifests. For decades the entertainment industry has made money off the dream of the happy home. From the sounds of "Fibber McGee and Molly," through the decades of "Leave It To Beaver" and "Father Knows Best," to the '70s when the dream began to crack and we turned back the pages of time to what we perceived as happier days, we longed for our homes to be like theirs. Homes like those of "The Waltons" and "Little House on the Prairie" were filled with laughter, stable relationships, love and affection, where conflict was quickly resolved. In the '80s we clung to the Huxstables of "The Cosby Show" and the Keatons of "Family Ties" to show us how to live together. We still envy their communication skills, the way they express themselves, love their parents and teach their children. From them we received a vision of what home life should be.

In reality, however, many homes today are "dysfunctional," a medical term combining the Greek prefix *dys* meaning "poor or bad" with the word *functional*, meaning "capable of operating or performing well." When we are not like the model home, we feel a sense of shame: It is another arena in which we don't quite measure up. So up goes the mask and into the pool of addictions and compulsions we dive to drown our sorrow.

As divorce breaks the unity of a family, children are shuffled between two homes and forced to live sometimes under often opposing sets of moral values. But the broken home is not the only dysfunctional home. Addictions all have destructive impacts on the family causing all attention, either conscious or subconscious, to be showered on the addicted family member. As we will describe in detail in chapter 8, the family members in a dysfunctional home operate by a hidden set of laws such as "Don't look at the problem," "Don't change it" and "Keep to yourself." As a result, the family members adopt distinct roles. In these ways, the family keeps its dark secrets hidden from public scrutiny and even denies the presence of the addictions that make it sick from within. There is no such thing as a healthy, normal family where addiction exists.

Nor is the Christian family a stranger to dysfunction. Wayne Kritsberg, family addiction counselor and author of *The Adult Children of Alcoholics Syndrome: From Discovery to Recovery*, describes four types of alcoholic families. Type 2 is one of the most frequently found forms of dysfunctional homes in the Church. He writes, "In this alcoholic family system, the actively drinking member of the nuclear family has stopped drinking. Although the active alcoholism has been arrested, the family system will continue to operate in a way that can only be described as alcoholic." Unless it is discovered and treated, it will continue to operate by the same dysfunctions, the same hidden sets of laws and roles, as the home where active alcoholism is present.

Pastors must no longer teach just the biblical ideal of the healthy home, but must address with compassion the problems of the dysfunctional home. Does our traditional interpretation of submission hold true when substance/process addictions bring on sexual and physical abuse? What are we teaching that will minimize the risk of vulnerability to quick-fix mood-altering substances and processes? The temptations created by living in an addictive society and a dysfunctional home need desperately the healing touch of Christ through His Church. But often when hurting people turn to the Church what they find is an extension of the dysfunctional family.

The Dysfunctional Church

Seeing unfortunate happenings in the Church, the third institution actually contributing to addiction, does not suggest a lack of love for her. The Church is the Body for which Jesus poured out His life and blood. He watches over her with an eternal commitment and pours out upon those able to receive it, lavish manifestations of His grace and power. She is His only plan for spreading the Gospel to a lost world and the only suitable container for His generations of harvests. The Church will go on until His coming when she will glow in bridal attire and rise to meet her faithful Lord. The local church, the expression of Christ's Body in every place, is to be a healing home in which the sick and hurting can be restored to emotional and spiritual health.

All too often, however, churches are full of wounded people, the products of dysfunctional homes who themselves have never been healed and, therefore, reproduce after their kind emotionally dysfunctional and spiritually stunted members. Carrying their hidden rules into church, Christians create the same problems with communication and stable relationships. The unhealthy solutions they learned in the home are often applied to situations in the Body of Christ, resulting in broken fellowship and much hurt. Church-hopping becomes the norm as the dysfunctional person isolates himself and discards relationships with those who disappoint him, ever searching for the perfect church and the perfect pastor.

The Rev. Stephen Apthorp, an Episcopal priest and director of Alcoholism and Substance Abuse Prevention in Tucson, Arizona, conducts regional training seminars for Christian clergy and lay leaders on the subject of chemical dependency. Apthorp has observed several startling facts about the effects of alcoholism and chemical dependency on church leaders and their congregations. More than eighty percent of the clergy attending his seminars are from dysfunctional homes themselves and admit that their home lives affected their decisions to enter the ministry. The lay leaders attending his seminars say that "they looked to their churches and clergy for help, support and God's affirming love. Ironically, in so doing they often put their trust in dysfunctional people and places."

Apthorp goes on to note in an article for *The Christian Century* that a common observation among chemical dependency counselors is this: People who grew up in dysfunctional families attract and are drawn to others who grew up in such families. "Therefore," he writes, "impaired pastors often collect impaired parishioners. No wonder that the Church at large, and the clergy in particular, have difficulty recognizing and dealing with today's epidemic affliction of addiction."

If the Church is to be a healthy representation of Christ, she must become a forum of honesty where sham can be dropped and the healing balm of Jesus Christ can be applied with grace and power. But many times the naïve Christian expects perfection and is not prepared to experience the shattered dream all over again.

Jason was one for whom the dream was shattered. A handsome, red-haired boy, Jason grew up in a reasonably happy home, the only child of a small-town pastor. Jason's parents loved and disciplined him and tried their best to give him what he needed and wanted. But Jason lived secretly with a throbbing emotional hurt.

When Jason was a preteen, he was friends with several children in the church. They were in Jason's life from the time they were in the nursery together until it was nearly time for high school. That is when the trouble erupted. When his father announced the board's decision to construct a new church building, factions began marshaling forces. Disagreements over size, location, decor and even whether or not building was the right decision began to rock the fellowship. Jason was caught in the middle and attempted to maintain friendships with the sons of disgruntled members, but to no avail.

One by one, Jason watched all his friends leave the church with their parents until he had no one left in whom he could confide. Worse yet, several of his friends betrayed Jason's confidence by revealing "juicy tidbits" about the personal life of Jason's family to their angry parents, which only fueled the conflagration.

Jason survived the summer alone, but when school started, it was a group of misfits that began to invite him to hang out. It was then that he was introduced to his first "hit" of cocaine. He never intended it to mushroom into addiction; he hoped only to find relief from the pain of loneliness and isolation that had set in. In his heart he had always trusted Jesus Christ, but unable now to get in touch with the God he felt had let him down, he started a long journey into the tunnel of addiction.

Jason's story should be rare, but it isn't and won't be as long as Christians raised in hurting homes are blind to the root of their problems. It's "not my brother, not my sister, but it's me, O Lord, standin' in the need of prayer. Not the pastor, not the deacon, but it's me, O Lord, standin' in the need of prayer."

The Quick Fix

The addictive society, the dysfunctional home and the dysfunctional church unwittingly cooperate to create a breeding ground for addiction. In order to mask pain and make up to ourselves for failures to meet perfectionistic expectations, we turn to mood-alterers for a quick fix. It is easier to shop than to allow ourselves to feel. It is easier to drink than to risk failure, easier to snort cocaine than to live life without it and far easier to "eat, drink and be merry" than to consider eternal realities. We do dope because we can't cope.

Christians use mood-alterers in the same way as the world but often with more acceptable substances and processes. While we would not admit it if we drank, we gorge ourselves at church covered-dish dinners and chase down the food with gulps of caffeine. Christian women who would never get high on anything else often numb their pain or relieve their boredom with compulsive shopping. The adult children of dysfunctional homes immerse themselves in compulsive work, slaving long hours into the night to avoid the discomfort of awkward relationships.

We live in an addictive society, believing in the "dream" only to have it shattered by reality. As it was for the descendants of Jacob, so it is for the addict. Egypt promises what it cannot deliver and lures the unsuspecting into a world in which he cannot cope and to which he must eventually surrender as a slave. It is the addictive society's belief in the dream of "more," "better" and "perfection" that sets up its members as vulnerable prey for the addictive cycle, a predictable process that we will examine in the following chapter.

4
The Tornado of Addiction

The shape of an addiction is something like a tornado. To begin, as we have already seen, the climate must be right for addiction to develop. Tornadoes usually develop when a cold air mass collides with a warm air mass. The addictive society, the hurting home and the hurting church provide the climate, but it is the introduction of the mood-alterer into the environment that sets the addictive cycle in motion, as it did in the case of Mary Sue.

Mary Sue had been brought up in a Christian home in which colorful clothes, jewelry and cosmetics were prohibited. While the other girls wore the latest styles, Mary Sue was clad in baggy dresses of drab colors. In her physical education class, she was the only girl not permitted to wear shorts and was obligated instead to wear a white skirt that dipped to mid-calf length. All the other girls looked upon Mary Sue as a religious prisoner. She felt like an "ugly duckling" in a school of "swans." Mary Sue was fourteen when she made up her mind that once she was on her own, she would never again feel ugly.

When Mary Sue was graduated from high school, she went to secretarial school and finished high in her class. Landing a good job, she determined to ignore the objections of her family and church, and to shed her drab cocoon and be transformed into a butterfly. Her first trip to the mall was a dream. She had her colors analyzed and her hair and makeup done professionally. She combed the stores for jeans, dresses, blouses and skirts. Next came accessories—brightly colored scarves, leather and suede belts and expensive costume jewelry. She stopped at the earring store and had her ears pierced. Before the day was over she had spent her paycheck, but basked in the rush of excitement brought by all her new purchases.

Several weeks went by. As she enjoyed the compliments of her colleagues at work and the double-takes of men on the street, Mary Sue vowed never to return to her religiously fanatical garb of the past. One Saturday she felt bored. With nothing else to do, she remembered the fun of her last shopping spree. Returning to the mall she signed up at all the department stores and shops for credit cards in order to be able to take advantage of the sales. She couldn't resist charging a few things on the cards that permitted instant credit.

As the months passed, Mary Sue began to get deeper and deeper into debt. Whenever she felt lonely, bored or tired, a trip to the mall picked her up. Each time she silenced the inner voice warning her of financial disaster. Before she knew it, she was thousands of dollars in debt and her wardrobe took up the entire walk-in closet in her apartment. But regardless of her bulging dresser drawers and packed closet, during every free moment at work, she began to be preoccupied with thoughts of other outfits she could buy.

Mary Sue felt guilty at the new church she attended whenever the offering was taken. Her money was so tied up with debts that she felt she couldn't afford to tithe, and each time the offering plate was passed, she looked the other way. She was already looking for a second part-time job to help pay her bills. By the time she asked her pastor for prayer and counseling, she was in despair—and deep debt.

How Addiction Develops

Mary Sue did not realize that the climate of her childhood was a perfect setup for addiction to develop. Her home environment, although Christian, was devoid of affection and affirmation. Her mother was so busy caring for her four younger brothers and sisters that Mary Sue was forced into a coparenting role and had little time just to be a child herself. Her father's perfectionist expectation of his family manifested itself in religious ways. Mary Sue never *felt* her parents' approval and developed instead a sense of rejection that manifested itself in a desire to prove her worth to herself and others.

The church Mary Sue attended as a young person also contributed to her addictive environment. Its stringent codes of dress were expounded regularly from the pulpit and the desire to dress like the crowd was denounced as sinful. Makeup and earrings were condemned. And yet Mary Sue saw that other girls her age, members of other churches, loved Jesus Christ and were able to dress fashionably and modestly at the same time. Her church emphasized externals as the true marks of Christianity, rather than the hidden virtues of the heart. What resulted was the reverse of what the church intended to happen. Mary Sue broke away from her church because it was isolated from the society it wanted so much to influence.

It was into this environment that Mary Sue introduced the element of the mood-alterer. In her case it was shopping. Whenever she was under stress or emotional pain, she turned to the mall as an alcoholic would turn to the bottle. Unaware of the addictive cycle, she fell prey to it easily. Gradually her desire to have her mood altered increased, as did her appetite for beautiful clothes. Soon she crossed over into lust for them, becoming preoccupied and obsessed with the desire for more, planning what she would buy after work each day.

Then came the phase of denial. In Mary Sue's case the voice of her conscience warning her to slow down was passed off as "bondage." Denial plunged her into ever-deepening absorption in her shopping habit. In time, guilt and remorse over her expenditures began to replace the original excitement. When her colleagues joked about her shopping their comments were met with defensiveness until she began to hide her new purchases to avoid remarks. Her shame plunged her into despair, the sense of hopelessness common to all addicts.

The Addictive Cycle

Mary Sue's story can be repeated by every addict using different substances and processes. Each tale of addiction follows the same cycle, a whirlwind process repeated within different spans of time. If addiction is to be subdued in a person's life, the addictive cycle must be interrupted. Learning the stages of the cycle, therefore, can reveal to the addict and those close to him when he is most vulnerable to being sucked into its spiral.

The stages of this cycle are the following:

1. Stress

The constricting of the throat, nervousness, irritability, exhaustion, frustration and anxiety begin to build. These symptoms may be caused by positive or negative influences. The pressure of the job or the elation of accomplishing a goal can induce stress on the mind and body. Broken relationships contribute to man's deepest hidden fear, the fear of abandonment. As stress builds the addict knows only one way of coping: turning to his mood-alterer.

2. Contemplation

At the subconscious level, the addict begins to contemplate the need for his mood-alterer. At this stage, craving is minimal, but it is sure to increase as the cycle progresses. Gradually the thought becomes a conscious one as he remembers the pleasure of past experiences and the relief it brought him.

3. Obsession

During this stage the addict finds it difficult to concentrate on matters at hand because he is obsessed with the thought of his mood-alterer. Access to the mood-alterer becomes a priority. Craving, which began during the contemplation stage, becomes overwhelming and moves quickly into the next stage of the addictive cycle, compulsivity.

4. Compulsivity

During the compulsivity phase, the addict's body begins to commit itself to indulgence. It is this phase that becomes humiliating to the addict. "It is as if a power greater than myself overwhelms me and pushes me into the motions of my addiction," cried one sex addict. Like a plane on automatic pilot that cannot be switched off, the rational mind, the moral convictions, the conscious choice are all shut down and the addict is now propelled by the motion, the ritual. This ritual is particular to each type of addict. The cocaine addict hits the street looking for his dealer, stops at nothing to ensure he has the money, purchases regardless of the danger and returns to a private place. For a food addict to fulfill his craving it is little different.

5. Indulgence

By this time, the craving is so overwhelming that the addict cannot stop. Like a zombie in a horror movie, the addict enters a state of mind totally preoccupied with his indulgence. The temptation to O.D., to gulp down large quantities of booze, eat whole pies, gamble away savings, buy more clothes or work all night consumes him. During this stage, the addict frequently violates his own moral principles or breaks the promise he has made to himself that he will stop. When the addict awakens to the reality of what he has done, he enters the next phase of the addictive cycle.

6. Remorse

Because he has disappointed himself, the addict becomes remorseful. Guilt over the fact that he has not been able to keep his promise to himself and to those he loves overwhelms him. He feels degraded and is fearful of being discovered and of the consequences he faces for his actions.

7. Denial

Unable to cope with his guilt and the consequences of his indulgence, the addict enters denial, the delusion that his indulgence is only an isolated incident, not a true addiction. In this stage he has the illusion of control. He straightens his tie, shaves and goes out to buy his wife a gift to make up for any unpleasantries he caused the night before. If he is a Christian, he repents of his sinful act. In this way he bolsters his sense of self-worth. He attempts to rationalize his participation in the addictive cycle and makes new promises to himself and others that he will never do "that" again. This false sense of power over his addiction only sets him up as prey for phase one of the addictive cycle, stress. Without the humility of realizing his powerlessness, he is left unprotected and vulnerable to repeating the cycle, once again turning to his mood-alterer.

Common Mood-Alterers

Under stress, vulnerable people turn to various substances and processes to bring relief and are sucked into the addictive tornado.

Christians are not immune to the need for mood-alterers. The same boredom, the same emotional pain, the same trials and temptations and the same appetites are present in all men who walk through this world. Paul and Peter found it necessary to urge believers to overcome the works of the flesh.

Paul's letters to the churches at Rome, Corinth, Ephesus, Thessalonica and Colossae, as well as his fatherly advice to Timothy and Titus, include exhortations toward purity. His advice to Rome majors on the theme of overcoming enslavement to lusts and pleasures. In the book of Revelation, the apostle John calls the members of the seven churches to repentance in the face of the Second Coming of the Lord Jesus Christ. What had happened to the revival in the book of Acts that caused the unbelievers to look upon the early Church as a jewel of power, grace and holiness?

When the initial burst of power that accompanies the entrance of the Holy Spirit in the life of the believer begins to subside, there is usually the temptation to fill the seeming void with other activities that will soothe the emotions. These mood-alterers can gradually consume a person's life and replace the throne of Christ. Not even the apostle Paul believed he was immune to this human dilemma. "For the good that I wish, I do not do," he wrote, "but I practice the very evil that I do not wish" (Romans 7:19). It is because of this paradox, the new spirit trapped in a corruptible, "addictable" body, that the Christian remains vulnerable to addiction.

You are about to meet more brothers and sisters in Christ who are facing painful struggles with addictions of various kinds. If you are addicted yourself, perhaps you will be able to see your own destructive patterns. It is a snare many of us have been caught in.

The names and details in the stories have been purposely changed to protect anonymity; any resemblance to people you know is coincidental. Other examples are drawn from the misery of public Christians whose names and faces have found their way into the national media. It is not my intent to magnify their pain, but to use their trials to point all of us to greater liberty in Christ. All of these members of the family of God, the public and anonymous, some who have been thrust into the light and others who have bravely stepped into the light, preach through their lives a message of warning and hope to others caught in bondage.

Many of these addicts fell into addiction before they ever met Jesus Christ. The fact that they have acknowledged and sought help for their addictions indicates the presence of the Holy Spirit doing a gentle cleansing work in their lives. As He slowly loosens and removes one chain after another, they find greater and greater measures of freedom. They are to be applauded.

Some of these Christian addicts got into trouble after their new birth experiences by trying to replace old problems with an addiction or to ease emotional pain. Others are still in various stages of denial, unable to face their addictions out of fear. Neither do these deserve condemnation and judgment, but our earnest prayers for healing and recovery.

How to find healing and recovery is the major focus of the second section of this book, but before we see the solution to addiction, it is necessary to examine its many seductive forms that can keep us bound. Perhaps you are already wondering whether or not a "habit" you have is really an addiction. Take a moment to answer the questions in the following quiz for some enlightenment.

Is It Habit or Addiction?

Test yourself by answering yes or no to the following questions. (Be honest!)

_____ 1. Do I turn to my habit when I'm under positive or negative stress?

_____ 2. Do I need more of the substance or activity than I used to in order to experience pleasure?

_____ 3. Do I turn to my substance or habit as a reward?

_____ 4. Do I feel the need to hide my substance or activity from those who know me?

_____ 5. Has my habit affected my productivity at all on the job or at home?

_____ 6. Have I stolen, overextended my credit or used money designated for other budget needs to support my habit?

_____ 7. If left unchecked, could my habit be destructive to myself or others?

_____ 8. Have those closest to me mentioned my excesses to me?

_____ 9. Do I feel defensive when the subject of my habit is brought up?

_____10. Do I feel guilt or remorse for indulging in my habit?

_____11. Do I promise myself I will stop?

_____12. Do I find that, regardless of my resolve to stop, I turn to it again?

_____13. Do I plan activities, reject or accept invitations on the basis of the availability of my substance or habit?

_____14. Do I indulge when I am alone?

_____15. Do I indulge at times others would call odd?

_____16. Has indulging in my habit brought emotional pain, physical injury or quenched the Holy Spirit in myself or others?

Score: Remember that no single test can offer definitive proof or results. Use this and every test in this book to help you determine whether or not you or someone you know might benefit from seeking further help. With that in mind, figure scores this way:

Answering yes to numbers 1, 3 and 7 could indicate a habit in the beginning stages of addiction. At this stage it is important to keep it in check and not let it develop further. Answering yes to any of the others could indicate that the addiction has progressed to the point that it would benefit from counseling, a support group and/or a treatment center.

If you are still not sure whether or not the action concerning you is an addiction, the next two chapters will unravel more details of addiction's many subtle forms. Let's begin by taking a look at the first category of addictions, addiction by mouth, and its relation to those in the Church.

5
In the Church: Addiction by Mouth

Sam Fitzgerald fell at the altar weeping at the end of the service, his first day back at church after ten years of backsliding. His wife was overjoyed to see Sam recommit himself to Jesus Christ. Not long afterward, Sam and June opened their house to prayer meetings and their phone lines to counseling needs. The pastor of Sam and June's church was delighted to see the fervor of their commitment and frequently held them up as examples of the Lord's power to transform.

What the pastor did not know was that Sam's ten-year period of backsliding was a result of alcoholism. He had lost his license to drunk driving violations and had broken up a previous marriage because of his drinking. So, when June reported a year and a half later that Sam had received a traffic citation for drunk driving, but had repented, the pastor passed it off as an isolated incident.

As months went by, Sam changed jobs frequently. He was impatient with his employers who, according to Sam, asked him to violate his conscience. Sam was impulsive in his decision-making and impatient with the failings of others. When Sam left the church several months later, the pastor was dismayed. Not long afterward Sam was ordered by a judge to attend A.A. in the face of more drunk driving violations. Only then did it become clear that Sam was an alcoholic.

Alcoholism

Dr. Anderson Spickard, medical director at the Vanderbilt Institute for Treatment of Alcoholism, elder in his Presbyterian church and co-author of *Dying for a Drink*, writes, "It can happen in any church, but it is the rare congregation that knows the extent of its drinking problem. Because church members often fail to distinguish between drunkenness and addiction, and because alcoholics are viewed in a judgmental and moralistic light, many Christians mistakenly believe that their fellow believers are immune from the danger of addiction. This conviction allows them to overlook even the most obvious symptoms of alcoholism, particularly if they appear in a Sunday school teacher, a deacon or a minister."

The symptoms of alcoholism are usually passed off as backsliding when actually the alcoholic is in relapse. Sam's incidents of drunk driving, his previously broken marriage, his judgmental attitude, his compulsive decision-making and his frequent job-changing are all symptoms of addictive behavior. Unless the pattern is observed, the alcoholism remains undiagnosed and untreated.

What are other symptoms of alcoholism? Stephen Arterburn, in *Growing Up Addicted*, quotes an article by F. Lemere in the *American Journal of Psychiatry* entitled "The Nature and Significance of Brain Damage from Alcoholism": "In working with thousands of alcoholics, I've seen only one characteristic that they all had in common: the ability to consume large quantities of alcohol." High tolerance, the ability to "drink 'em under the table," is actually a symptom of alcoholism. The alcoholic has developed an increased need of the depressant to produce the same effects.

Other symptoms include memory losses, blackouts, withdrawal pains such as D.T.s, secondary diseases such as cirrhosis of the liver, pancreatitis and arthritis, and behavioral changes including personality changes, poor job performance, loss of work time and the inability to stop drinking permanently.

Dr. Arterburn also points out that recent medical discoveries indicate that alcoholics metabolize alcohol differently from other drinkers. When an alcoholic ingests alcohol, part of the acetaldehyde is retained in his brain tissue where it undergoes chemical changes and transforms into a chemical abbreviated THIQ. This substance is eight times more addictive than morphine and is known to remain in the brain seven years after the last drink. It is responsible for the return of the craving to drink. This piece of information alone is enough to relieve the Christian alcoholic who all along has thought, in spite of his spiritual disciplines, that his craving to drink was only the result of sin or moral failure.

Some 95 percent of all alcoholics are not skid-row bums but respectable people who hold jobs and have families. They are functional alcoholics whose alcoholism has not yet progressed to the point of complete debilitation. Not all alcoholics get drunk every day either. Binge alcoholism, one of the more prominent forms of alcoholism, gives the alcoholic the illusion of control. The binge alcoholic may go for ten days, six weeks or 25 years without getting drunk, only to snap back to it in time of stress for no other explained reason.

It is this form of alcoholism that caught Christian singer Chuck Girard in its cruel snare. The November 1989 issue of *Charisma* magazine told Chuck's story showing that it is possible to be a high-profile Christian and an alcoholic, unable to control oneself. Chuck revealed in his courageous testimony how social drinking had led him back into the bondage of alcoholism after he was saved and traveling on the gospel music circuit. While his albums soared to the top of the Christian charts, he was sinking fast into the depths of bondage to alcoholism. Through the insistence of his wife, Chuck found help in a treatment center and, at this writing, has been drug- and alcohol-free for more than a year and a half.

Not all alcoholics drink enough to get drunk but find themselves dependent on low-dosage alcohol. One A.A. member reports the rise in attendance among men and women who have discovered they cannot stop the daily habit of a "social" drink at a business lunch.

It is important for every church to wake up to the presence of alcoholism in its members. It is a powerful physical addiction with disease-like symptoms that run a fatal course. As much as a diabetic must avoid overeating, the alcoholic must avoid anything—even medications—that contains alcohol. It is also imperative that the Church be aware of the symptoms a "dry" alcoholic manifests before he is about to relapse, which we will note in a later chapter.

Drug Addiction

According to Peter Jennings on ABC's "World News Tonight" (September 5, 1989), a recent poll indicates that 33 percent of Americans have tried illegal hard drugs at least once. Who would have thought we would ever see stock brokers on Wall Street file out after the closing bell to buy cocaine on the street corner? Or see cocaine in candy bowls at cocktail parties? Or teen drug traffickers driving Corvettes with thousands of dollars' worth of gold jewelry around their necks? The Church, like a dry sponge soaking up the trends of society, is also soaking up drug addiction.

Jason, the pastor's son introduced in chapter 3, became addicted during a period of disillusionment with the Church. With "crack cocaine," the instantly addictive drug easily available on the streets of every city in America, the Church's youth are a pushover the first time they sow a single wild oat.

But the church youth group is not the only part of the Church in danger. One of the most common forms of drug addiction among Christians is the addiction to tranquilizers and other over-the-counter prescriptions.

Roy, who had a history of angina, had been a Christian for three years when he found the church he had been looking for—a small pioneer work in a suburb of Baltimore. Committing himself to the fellowship fully, Roy believed, as did the rest of the congregation, that he had truly been sent by God on a mission to help the struggling church. Roy gave great testimony to the love and joy of the Lord, brightening every meeting he attended—and he rarely missed a single one. Although he was an older man, he made friends easily among the young people. He had never married but enjoyed female company. Since he was not well enough to hold down a job, Roy spent his days at home chatting by phone with the housewives of the church. He enjoyed this "counseling ministry," and often called to cheer up the downcast.

When Roy again began to suffer from angina pains, he

sought medical attention. No one noticed, however, that he began to consult several doctors about the same ailment. He never seemed to be without a fresh bottle of percodan and took it frequently "to relieve his pain." Roy was also a heavy smoker. He coughed and reeked of tobacco. Everyone vacillated between love and pity for Roy, and when he was in the hospital, his room was always full of members of the congregation encircling his bed.

But Roy was not always a saint. He enjoyed being argumentative about trivial matters. He would locate some obscure verse and argue a position to the point of anger. Roy finally left his church after one of those arguments, but the congregation was relieved. He had more than once been the center of a gossip ring. What Roy and the church never realized was that he was a drug addict, a percodan "junkie."

Jo Anna is a born-again Christian, mother of four toddlers, married to a workaholic corporate executive and living in a lovely suburban home. She came forward for prayer after a women's meeting to confess to me her anguish over her valium addiction. Jo Anna explained that as her supply would be depleted, she would contact several doctors in different parts of the city to ensure that enough prescriptions were filled. She was afraid her husband—unsympathetic to anyone unable to control himself—would find out and the marriage would dissolve.

During the recent PTL scandal, we learned of Tammy Faye Bakker's addiction to prescription drugs. The hectic, glamour-filled lifestyle of media ministry had proven to be for her, as it is for the secular entertainer, a perfect breeding ground for addiction.

The problem of drug addiction in the Church will inevitably increase as new believers are harvested from an addictive society. If the revival many predict occurs soon, our churches will be loaded with drug addicts and alcoholics in fragile states of recovery, and we must be ready. But in order to be ready, the Church must learn to deal with other debilitating addictions, more subtle because of their social acceptance. These are food, nicotine and caffeine.

Food Addiction

Agnes had always been a faithful member of her Methodist church, singing in the choir and teaching a primary girls' Sunday school class for more than eight years. She had accepted Christ at a youth fellowship meeting as a teenager and, from then on, never missed a Sunday, even riding the church bus when her family wouldn't go.

Agnes had never considered taking alcohol or drugs because "nice girls didn't do such things." She did, however, battle her weight constantly. By the time she was a high school graduate, she was buying clothes from the large-size shops. And Agnes never had a date.

It was not as though Agnes had not tried to stop overeating. She realized early in her Christian life that food controlled a large part of her thought life. Determined to use her strong willpower on her appetite, Agnes tried every new diet she heard of. But after a few weeks, she always regained the weight. She confessed the sin of idolatry about food whenever messages were preached about self-control, but once out of the church sanctuary, she found it hard to resist the smell of French fries at the Dairy Queen down the street.

As Agnes approached her mid-forties, she became depressed, losing almost all interest in her appearance and withdrawing into a shell. Her friends didn't see her much anymore because she drove to work and to church and hardly anywhere else. Lonely times were frequent, and she absorbed herself in a fantasy world of romance novels and cable TV. On the coffee table were always several packages of chips and cartons of dip. She went to restaurants alone and assured herself that the Lord wanted her to have some pleasure in life. Each meal amounted to approximately 3,000 calories: salad bar, steak, baked potatoes with mountains of sour cream and butter, fried zucchinis on the salad bar and, of course, a chocolate sundae.

Sometimes Agnes knew exactly what she was eating, but at other times she just ate to be eating—to pass the lonely hours. Her taste buds demanded and got whatever morsel they wanted. After each binge she felt remorse and guilt. It was after one such binge, in which she consumed a large chocolate cake in one sitting, that Agnes finally went to her doctor. He had disturbing news. Her cholesterol level was over 300 mg/dl and her blood-sugar count indicated the onset of diabetes. The results of her physical exam hit her hard. The motivation to lose weight was no longer cosmetic—it was now a matter of life and death.

Food addiction follows the same progression as any other substance addiction, and it is the most common addiction in the Church. One of the culture shocks missionaries experience upon returning to America is the sight of masses of overweight people. We are the fattest nation on the face of the earth. The nation's top two killers, cancer and heart disease, are linked to food addiction. But food addiction has several different manifestations.

Compulsive overeating is not the only form of food addiction. Victims of anorexia nervosa, the eating disorder that causes loss of appetite, include the late popular singer Karen Carpenter, who slowly starved herself to death as her family watched in horror. Nor is it a stranger in the Church. In *Starving for Attention* Cherry Boone O'Neill, daughter of entertainer Pat Boone, tells of her ten-year battle with anorexia. At the peak of her disease, she did such things as count the calories in the Communion elements, shoplift laxatives from stores and eat dinner scraps in the dog's dish. Her fear of gaining weight drove her to exercise several hours a day, lie to her family, hide her binges and vomiting—and nearly destroy her marriage.

In *Overcoming Overeating,* Jane R. Hirschmann and Carol H. Munter make the following observation: "The dual preoccupation with food and body shape is the hallmark of compulsive eating. Some compulsive eaters submit to their need for food and eat. Others control their desire for food and diet. In either case, the addiction to food rules the life of the compulsive eater."

In addition to the more obvious eating disorders like bulimia and anorexia, "wrong eating" which drives its victims to eat foods that cause and aggravate existing medical problems is another form of compulsive eating. Sugar addiction (a common problem for recovering alcoholics) and chocolate addiction (which combines two chemical addictions, caffeine and sugar) tempt the Christian probably more frequently than any other kind. In their book *The Hidden Addiction and How to Get Free* two medical doctors, Janice Keller Phelps and Alan E. Nourse, theorize that sugar addiction—or carbohydrate dysmetabolism—is the key factor present in all other substance addictions. In their opinion, the person whose system dysmetabolizes carbohydrates is most likely to develop alcoholism and other addictions.

The Church, which often adopts a self-righteous attitude toward alcoholism and drug addiction, looks the other way at food addiction. Yet these addicts center church activities around the presence of their drug of choice—food—and eat themselves to death. Food addiction is as fatal as alcoholism. It is another way of destroying the temple of the Holy Spirit. And even though it is frequently exposed in Scripture along with drunkenness as leading to destruction, it is viewed, sadly, in some churches as just a more acceptable way of hiding emotional pain.

Nicotine

"It is hard to imagine Jesus smoking a cigarette," said Freda, a longtime smoker. "But to me, cigarettes were harder to give up than marijuana and alcohol." Freda was not addicted to marijuana and alcohol, but was addicted to nicotine.

Like other addictions, this one will kill. Aside from the overwhelming risk of developing lung cancer, a smoker is four times more likely to have a heart attack than a nonsmoker. But in the face of these facts, many Christians continue to smoke because they cannot quit with willpower alone. Another longtime Christian smoker told me, "I haven't smoked in twenty years, but sometimes the craving is so strong, I have the urge to pick up old cigarette butts off the parking lot and light up!"

I grew up in the Bible belt. Every Sunday outside the church door, the odor of tobacco smoke mingled with the scent of the sanctuary. My father read his Bible in his easy chair with a wad of Red Man in his jaw, and two of my uncles, one a Baptist deacon, smoked cigarettes. They all died of heart disease, my Uncle John at age 48 of a heart attack. Nicotine addiction is probably the second most common substance addiction in the Church. Driving through Virginia and the Carolinas, you see red brick churches with white columns springing up out of neatly cropped tobacco fields. Tobacco is a tradition in the South, and only politicians who support the industry are elected. Children start sneaking cigarettes in elementary school, lunchroom workers dip snuff in the cafeteria line and preachers smoke. And the devil laughs. At least he's found one way to destroy millions of Christians—cram tar into their lungs!

Caffeine

I hate to do it—I really do! But I can't let the nation's number one mood-alterer escape mention. Caffeine fills the coffeepots of adult Sunday school classes throughout America and the teapots of the United Kingdom. When we are bored, tired or depressed, we simply grab a Pepsi or turn on Mr. Coffee for a two-hour rush that propels us through the morning.

While caffeine has not been discovered to cause any major illnesses, it has been linked to increased instance of fibrocystic disease in women and aggravates heart disease and gastro-intestinal difficulties. It is a substitute high for many recovering addicts, but it subtly ruins their ability to be drug-free. It is also considered a trigger for the use of stronger drugs. Many drug and alcohol treatment centers are banning caffeine for addicts in treatment who need to learn to live life and experience their emotions without artificial inducement.

Although it is not considered a serious addiction, withdrawing from caffeine is not easy. Tapering off is generally recommended because those who try to go "cold turkey" usually return to it. Withdrawal symptoms include nausea, headaches, runny nose, depression and fatigue. In the words of one minister, "God has only put so many beats in my heart. Why use them up with caffeine?"

These are the major substance addictions that enslave the Church, but sadly there are more. Before we take a look at solutions, we will examine process addiction, an equally destructive form that I call "action" addiction. Action addictions suck the unsuspecting into the addictive cycle through the stimuli of activities. We cannot learn how to subdue addiction without taking a long, hard look at process addiction.

6
Action
Addictions

As we have seen so far, any recipe for addiction must include the following ingredients: (1) an addictive environment, (2) stress, usually pain, (3) one or more mood-alterers.

But not all mood-alterers are ingested. Some of the most powerful addictions do not involve alcohol, drugs or food, but are equally destructive. This group is called process addiction, or behavior addiction, in which the victim is caught in the tornado by repetitive, life-controlling behaviors. These processes include gambling, workaholism, compulsive worry, compulsive anger, shopping, entertainment, exercising and religious addiction, but there are others. The numbers of process addictions can be as numerous as the specialized interests of human beings, and are usually characterized by being healthy activities carried to unhealthy extremes.

For a person to be "action"-addicted, he must be on a destructive course, caught in the addictive cycle. And not all process addictions involve questionable moral behavior in the beginning. Even noble pursuits can turn into process addictions when they become all-consuming and uncontrollable, as in the case of Phil.

When Phil and his wife, Sandra, arrived at the counselor's office, they had been married a little over three years. Phil was the pastor of a mid-sized Presbyterian church in a neighboring town. An honors graduate in high school and a gridiron hero, Phil had graduated from college and seminary with high honors. Phil's parents had been killed in an automobile accident when he was a baby, and he had been reared by his grandparents who showered him with all the love and attention an only child could receive. In his second year of seminary, Phil had met and married Sandra, a music major, eager to use her talents to support Phil in his ministry.

Upon arriving at his first church after graduation, Phil was determined to be the best pastor the church ever had. He awakened at six A.M. and was at the church by seven where he spent an hour in prayer and meditation. The next eight hours were a whirl of Bible study, counseling and hospital visitation. Two nights a week the church had regularly scheduled services, but Phil, determined to see the church grow, spent long hours the other nights in pastoral visitation. Phil made it known that he could be reached any hour of the day or night.

Sandra, busy with choir practice and organ rehearsals while Phil made his nightly visits, was satisfied for a while, believing that Phil belonged to the Lord first and that her personal feelings had to be "laid on the altar." Months went by and most of the communication between Phil and Sandra came in the form of a quick good-bye kiss as the two passed each other on the front porch of the parsonage. It had been several months since they had eaten dinner without the interruption of a phone call from one of the parishioners about some business matter or prayer request. Phil missed the warning signs and was surprised when he arrived home and Sandra was not there. She had gone to visit her parents and left him a note saying, "Things have to change."

Workaholism

The circumstances of Phil's life were ripe for workaholism. As are most people who suffer from this action addiction, Phil was unaware of his vulnerability. Being reared by doting grandparents made it hard for Phil to be satisfied with being average. Although no active addict was present in Phil's home environment, his grandparents were both children of alcoholics and their homes had suffered from their dysfunctional desire to sacrifice themselves for others to the exclusion of their own needs. This desire had passed through the generations to Phil.

Phil's problem was complicated by a nagging fear that one day he would be left alone. Phil was not naturally affectionate and showing affection was mechanical for him. Although he loved Sandra deeply, he found it difficult, as many men do, to talk about feelings and to be intimate. Shoving all this into his subconscious mind, Phil tried to make up for his lack in expressing himself by throwing himself into his work. The admiration of the members of the congregation gradually replaced his lack of affirmation from Sandra, who was afraid to fuel his obsession with work by complimenting his sermons and his tireless sacrifice. Many of the older men in the church, workaholics themselves, were glad to see devotion to work as part of Phil's character. But Phil soon realized that once he had begun his ministry at a hectic pace, there was no way to let up for fear of disappointing those who had come to count on him.

Phil had learned to live with numb emotions and considered this the ideal emotional state, shielding himself from hurt by training himself never to react with emotion. He did not realize that in so doing, he shut out Sandra, too. As in the case of so many workaholics, the dream of a happy home is an impossible one. The home life becomes a sham with two people playing house while the children amuse themselves with little meaningful communication.

As in any other addiction, the workaholic always promises to stop. "After such and such date" or "when I get some help at work" or "after this one last project I'll quit." But he always violates his promise as a new activity needing his undivided attention emerges on the scene. This frustrates the spouse and children who feel guilty for demanding more of this awesome person's time.

When confronted about his excessive work, the workaholic will be as defensive as the alcoholic is about his drinking, insisting that he is a perfectly balanced individual, the ideal wife or the hard-working husband. Meanwhile, life's priorities are out of order, and he is headed on a destructive course deluding himself that he plans to stop. Christian workaholics who saturate their lives with service wind up using their God-ordained calling not to glorify God but to keep from facing life. Their ministries become their mood-alterers. Later we will see how people like Phil can overcome their activity addictions.

Gambling, Spending and Shopping

Flip is 29. His green eyes and charismatic personality charm everyone. For eleven years Flip has been a born-again Christian who attends services regularly. His life is happier now than it used to be. Flip grew up in a rough neighborhood, the son of a mentally ill father and a mother who died when Flip was a boy. To fill the void in his life, Flip hung out on the corner near the local cigar store. It was here that he met the men who molded his young life. The cigar store was the cover for the local bookie who started using Flip to run bets when he was only ten years old. As Flip grew older, he began making bets himself until he would bet on anything.

Determined to turn his back on the ghetto, Flip applied for financial aid, eventually graduated from a university and entered the business world. It was there that his gambling addiction resurfaced, this time in the form of high-risk business ventures and stock trading. He sat in front of the computer, downloading the latest stock information, caught up in the rush of buying, trading and selling. His TV was permanently tuned to the business network with the Dow-Jones averages running feverishly across the screen.

When Flip came to Jesus Christ, he stopped betting for a while on sports because he felt convicted that he was throwing away money. But his compulsion with the stock market kept the flames of addiction burning until eventually Flip realized he was hooked. He now attends Gamblers Anonymous and is in treatment, but he nearly lost his wife and family to his gambling addiction.

The desire for money is secondary to the compulsive gambler. The "high" comes from risking all, courting financial disaster. The story was told in *Time* magazine (July 10, 1989) of Karen, a 42-year-old compulsive gambler who started going to Las Vegas casinos early in her marriage. She began to lose touch with the needs of her family, until an incident occurred that caused her husband to realize she was addicted: Her children were left in the rain, locked out of the house, waiting for her while she placed one more bet.

In the same article, Dr. Howard Shaffer of Harvard's Center for Addiction Studies estimated that the proportion of American adults who bet at least occasionally has risen from sixty percent to eighty percent in the past twenty years. Betting has reached into our churches. Bingo parlors, casino nights, raffles and church-sponsored lottery tickets are too much temptation for the compulsive gambler to bear.

Gambling addiction can be easily wrapped in a religious package labeled as "faith." Joe E. Barnhart and Steven Winzenburg, in their recent book about the PTL crisis, *Jim and Tammy*, explained that Jim Bakker viewed his fund-raising efforts as a Mexican cliff diver would eye the murky waters of a cove. As the cliff diver must time his impact to coincide with the swell of water, so Jim Bakker, moved by impulse, would announce to the public on Friday a grandiose project requiring funds the ministry did not have. Invariably, the money would come in by the following week from avid supporters who admired his cliff dives of "faith."

The pressure of the ministry Jim Bakker created, the emotional and physical exhaustion of TV appearances and the high of plunging into one risky venture after another were enough to hurl him into the process-addictive cycle. The victims of Jim's actions included not only himself and his family, but a large sector of the Body of Christ who lavished millions on Jim's word that his expenditures were the will of God, as apparently he had come to believe they were.

Closely akin to gambling addiction is another process addiction that plunges its victims into debt. Mary Sue (introduced in chapter 4), who started shopping excessively when she left home and went out on her own, is now caught in the quagmire of compulsive shopping and has become a compulsive debtor.

Shopping Addiction

Shopping addiction masquerades as a hobby to many who fill lonely hours with this seemingly harmless amusement. But shopping and compulsive spending can turn into a financial nightmare as the victim becomes sucked in by the addictive cycle.

Following in the footsteps of shopaholic parents, the nation's young are gearing up for the big credit boom of the nineties. *U.S. News and World Report* reported (March 20, 1989) that "America's 25 million 'tweens—ages 9–16, those too old for Ronald McDonald, but too young to drive—influence the annual purchase of over $45 billion worth of goods." That's a lot of jeans and tennis shoes! The same article reported that psychologists see many parents who are alarmed by the warning signs of shopaholism in their children and are trying to intervene to break the addictive cycle.

But workaholism and shopaholism are not the only mood-alterers to which Christians turn in their hour of need. One of the most heartbreaking addictions for the addict, as well as for the victim, is sexual addiction.

Sexual Addiction

When I interviewed Christian counselor Glenda Moser, a well-known, certified addiction counselor in the Pittsburgh area, I tried to conceal my surprise when she revealed one of the Church's darkest secrets. One hundred percent of Glenda's clients are born-again Christians and forty percent of them are sex addicts. I shouldn't have been so surprised at this figure because, as a young girl, I—and several other girls— was victimized myself by a sex addict who was a deacon in one of the largest churches in town.

If recent surveys are correct, it is estimated that one out of every three women and one out of every six men have been sexually molested, many the victims of incest. Dr. Patrick J. Carnes, founder of the Golden Valley Health Center's program for sexual dependency in Minneapolis and author of *Out of the Shadows,* one of the foremost works on sexual addiction, divides the problem into three levels.

Level One sexual addicts participate in behavior that some facets of society consider acceptable, such as masturbation. They also have multiple sexual partners, are involved in prostitution and homosexuality. "Many Level One addicts believe they can control their behavior since it is not constant," explains Dr. Carnes. "They experience episodes in which they simply sexually binge. Then they stop for weeks or even months."

Level Two addictive behaviors include exhibitionism, those who expose themselves; voyeurism, which includes peeping toms, trips to porn shops, peep shows and movies; obscene phone calls; and inappropriate touches. Society regards these activities with disdain.

Level Three sex addicts participate in behaviors society considers to be vile. These include incest, child molestation, rape, violence, bestiality, sadomasochism and fetishism. At this level, the addiction graduates to a predatory form unleashing the addict's pent-up fury and frustration on a victim.

In all phases of sexual addiction, the illicit provides the thrill. The years 1987–1988 were not happy ones for evangelical and charismatic Christianity. The Body of Christ watched in dismay as the media took several of the nation's high-profile ministers to the woodshed. One of them was Jimmy Swaggart, a beloved televangelist. Swaggart had called Jim Bakker "a cancer that must be excised from the Body of Christ," yet he himself was exposed as what amounted to a Level Two sexual addict. *Time* magazine (March 7, 1988) reported that a high official in the Assemblies of God who attended the ten-hour session in Springfield, Missouri, where Swaggart confessed his indiscretions, said the well-known preacher told how he "had battled an obsession with pornography since his youth and had been a periodic backslider." Swaggart's obsession allegedly had led him to a prostitute who posed nude, the object of his voyeurism, at different times over a one-year period.

But the pressure of media ministry is not the only backdrop for sexual addiction. Floyd is the president of a small company that distributes farm machinery in the Midwest. A respected businessman and an officer in a local chapter of a Christian men's organization, Floyd's reputation for running a clean business remains unsoiled. Floyd has been married for 25 years and is the father of four children. No one would ever guess that Floyd's closet at work is filled with pornography, or that in the past five years many female employees have resigned because of his sexual harassment. Fear of scandal has silenced the women who put up with his flirtations. And yet Floyd denies that he has a problem, almost as though his indecent sexual activities are those of a person he doesn't know.

Hope for Healing

Perhaps you see someone you know in these pictures. There is hope. Addiction can be identified and overcome by a liberating process that involves the addict's cooperation, the help of others and the supernatural intervention of God—a process we will examine in detail.

Before healing can begin, though, we still have more to see that will help us detect addiction before it creates worse problems.

You may be asking, "Is there any way to recognize an addict before he becomes a threat to me, my family, my business, my church or himself? Are there addictive behaviors and personality traits that manifest in a pattern?"

In the next chapter, we will explore the effects of addiction on the mind and emotions, traits that cause the addict to stand apart from the crowd.

7
The Addict: A Slave and Oppressor

·The addict's journey into bondage scars not only his physical body, but his soul—his mind, will and emotions, causing him to be dysfunctional. The addictive cycle, to draw once more on our tornado image, sweeps over the addict, robbing him of his own life, freedom and happiness, and then uses him like a piece of whirling debris to destroy the lives of others. In this way, addiction cuts a swath through the landscape, uprooting relationships, exploding homes and destroying lives. Jack Mills stands out as one of the most destructive "storms" I have heard of.

Jack, a muscular, broad-shouldered assembly-line worker of Swedish stock, with blond hair, blue eyes and a winsome personality, was another who had been a heavy drinker before he was born again. His wife, Teresa, occasionally recalled the way Jack was before. After a tiring day at the auto works, Jack usually stopped by the neighborhood bar for a few drinks. When Jack wasn't drinking, he was fun to be around, laughing and joking with his friends; but when he *was* drinking, Jack became a wild boar on a rampage. He would stagger through the door loudly proclaiming his presence, while the two boys ran for their rooms and Teresa mustered the courage to face him.

One particular night couldn't be erased from Teresa's mind. Jack kicked in the door, bellowing obscenities. The boys ran to their rooms in fear as he grabbed Teresa and tore her clothes. In spite of her shrieks and pleas for mercy, he pushed her against the wall and raped her, slapping her while she cried. Finally he stumbled to his easy chair and demanded his dinner, leaving Teresa sobbing.

Jack and Teresa were both children of alcoholic parents, and they had grown up with more than their share of heartache. Teresa's father had left when she was a child. Teresa swore never to marry an alcoholic and repeat the mistakes her mother had made, but now, ten years later, she had.

When the neighborhood church held Vacation Bible School, Jack and Teresa's two boys began to attend. Teresa then began to attend the services and accepted Jesus Christ. Jack didn't follow immediately. Several more years of abusive drinking and intimidation passed, but Teresa prayed for him daily until finally a miracle happened.

While Teresa was gone one day, some of her church friends stopped by for a visit. Jack was watching TV with a beer in his hand but decided to be polite. Teresa's friends began to share with Jack about how Jesus wanted to save him, telling him about the love of God. He tried to bark at them with a comparatively mild obscenity, but they kept on. Jack's rough exterior began to soften, and before he knew it, he was on his knees begging God's forgiveness, crying and asking Jesus to save him.

When Teresa came home, Jack told her what had happened; she thought he was mocking her. But the next morning he got up, put on his only suit and went to church. He was later baptized and became active in the church, to the joy of everyone in the congregation.

Even though Jack had become a Christian, addiction had left its disfiguring scars on his family. Teresa, so often disappointed in the past, was still afraid of Jack, an attitude that began to eat at him. So were the boys, who avoided his attempts to show affection by pulling away. Jack was strong-willed and began to apply this trait to his Christian walk. Believing his alcoholism was a thing of the past, something that was gone forever, "under the blood of Jesus," as he liked to put it, he ignored the urging of his Christian friends to attend A.A., claiming the power of God had already done its work.

Jack was a natural leader who could rally people with a word. Always ready to express his opinions even though they were sometimes off-base, Jack found it easy to evangelize and tell others about the Lord. He soon rose to leadership in the church that brought him to Christ and was recognized as a sterling example of God's power to save "from the guttermost to the uttermost." In the congregational deacon's election, Jack received the most votes and was ordained a few weeks later.

Even before his ordination, though, Teresa began to experience reservations. Jack's behavior at home had been less than exemplary. His anger surfaced again; sometimes he bellowed so loudly the neighbors could hear him. He demeaned the boys with remarks that pierced like knives and would never apologize.

He bragged often about how hard he worked, but at work he was not averse to pilfering from the tool supply. When he didn't want to work, he called in sick, trusting in the power of the union to back him if his absences were ever questioned.

At church when it was time for work to be done, Jack was too busy. Soon he began to belittle the pastor behind his back and stir others to question the pastor's motives and methods. He frequently missed evening services because he said he had to spend time with his family, yet those evenings were spent in front of the TV. In deacons' meetings, he became abrasive.

People were afraid to challenge Jack because he gave the impression that he was always right. When Jack began to pressure the board of deacons to bring a constitutional change before the church that would diminish the pastor's role, the board said no. Unable to take this blow to his ego, Jack left the church for a new one. But when his attempts to control that church failed also, he gradually stopped going. It was then he took another drink. Today Jack is an active alcoholic. Jack's addiction left him an oppressor, a condition that was allowed to go on too long because it was both unrecognized and unchallenged.

Recognizing Addictive Behavior Before It's Too Late

The mistake made by Jack's church is common. The failure to discern addictive behavior and impending relapse in an addict accounts for much heartache. Failing to discern addiction is easy to do, especially for Christians who want, in love, to believe the best about brothers and sisters in Christ. Usually mistaken for sins of the flesh, addictive behavior can go undetected unless we learn to recognize the pattern. Taken alone, each symptom would cause little alarm, but when several symptoms begin to appear, an alarm bell should sound and spur us to action.

Addictive behavior does not develop overnight. Its roots are buried in basic attitudes that are the soil of an addiction. These beliefs make a person vulnerable to the need for a mood-alterer.

Slave-Mindedness

The heartfelt beliefs of addicts are not unlike those of the Hebrews who grew up in slavery in Egypt.

Centuries of seeing loved ones being used by the ruling class had affected them emotionally. So it is with the one who is used by the addictive cycle. The effect can be devastating. Let us examine the feelings and attitudes of those trapped in the slavery of addiction to attempt to understand their behavior.

1. *"I'm no good."*

The addict, enslaved because of his forced subservience, gradually adopts the attitude that he is less important than others. He is innately inferior, he thinks, which is why he is a slave. His apparent inability to rise to the level of those he serves quenches creativity, drive and feelings of worth. The repression of his value causes him to assert himself in trivial matters to prove his worth.

Jack's low sense of self-value manifested itself in his determination to assert his desires in every arena of his life. At home, he dominated his family; at church he took pride in his position and misused the authority he had been given; and on the job he felt the need to assert himself in taking what he could get from the company.

2. *"No one really cares about me."*

Because he is trapped in a situation out of his control, the slave fears being abandoned and clings to unhealthy relationships. The fear of abandonment persists in spite of the demonstrations of concern by others around him. Any adult who grew up in an alcoholic home, like the addict himself, is prone to the fear of abandonment because he had to parent himself. This fear prevents intimacy and promotes the desire to control circumstances by controlling people. This control and manipulation in ACOAs—Adult Children of Alcoholics—may take the form of overt domination or emotional manipulation of others as the addict silently withdraws.

Jack, the son of alcoholics, was tormented by the fear of abandonment, which manifested in the overwhelming need to control Teresa, his children, his friends at church and those on his job.

3. *"No one can be trusted."*

Akin to the fear of abandonment is the belief that no one can be trusted, that others will always fail. Many addicts have been hurt deeply by another whom they loved. For those brought up like that, it is a dog-eat-dog world in which everyone is out to survive. Relationships become secondary to survival; thus the view is promoted that *all* people are not trustworthy because they care only for themselves. What results is an attitude of fear and mistrust that closes the addict into a private den.

Jack was highly critical of everyone who did not allow him to control them. He bore a suspicious nature that caused him to mistrust the people who loved him most. He became suspicious of his pastor's motives because he had never been able to trust authority figures in his life. Both Jack and Teresa maintained a safe distance from others for fear of being disappointed and hurt, and yet Jack took all he could from those who had what he needed and wanted. Whenever relationships broke down, he sought to lay blame on the other party. In fact, his parting words to his pastor were, "You have totally ruined my Christian life."

4. "I'll always be this way."

When Moses finally led the Hebrews out of slavery, they had been in Egypt for 450 years. They felt they had no hope left. The addict, as well, is tortured with a fear that things will always be this way, that he is locked into his bondage forever. This produces rage. He is irritable and has a tendency toward angry outbursts.

5. "I must be perfect."

The addict's feelings of inferiority give way to the deception that he must be perfect. He becomes rigid in his beliefs and projects an air of self-righteousness. He must know all and do all. He demands that those he cares about be perfect, too. With him, it's all or nothing, black or white; the words *flexible* and *average* are not in his vocabulary. The addict sets a standard for himself that he cannot meet, which confirms his "I'm-no-good" belief. He wants to be free, to have a better life, but feels that he does not really deserve it because he cannot earn it, so he keeps turning to his addictive substance or action to relieve the stress. If you have ever lived with or been closely associated with an addict, you know how deeply frustrating his perfectionism can be to your own self-esteem.

6. *"I deserve to feel better."*

Unable to face the emotional stress caused by these wrong beliefs, the addict justifies his need for a mood-alterer by convincing himself he deserves to have his mood altered to soothe his emotional pain, relieve his boredom or fill his physical craving.

The dysfunctional behavior of the addict proceeds out of these wrong beliefs. These beliefs are not usually conscious thoughts, but constitute what psychologists call a running internal monologue that affects our emotions and behavior. Dr. William Backus, Christian psychologist and author of *Telling the Truth to Troubled People*, writes that "a feeling or an emotion is a result of what we are at the moment believing and telling ourselves from within. And a persistent, unwanted, negative emotion is our response to persistent repetition of certain beliefs in our internal monologue—repetition we may be only dimly aware is occurring." Wrong beliefs have the ability to enslave long after the physical chains have been removed. The following are the most common behavioral characteristics that proceed out of these wrong beliefs.

Behavioral Symptoms Common to Christian Addicts

1. *Denial*

The untreated addict will not be able to recognize powerlessness over his addiction. A binge addict, who is able to stop periodically, may begin to develop a false sense of self-control and deny the need to avoid contact with the addictive substance or process and those associated with it.

2. Cross-addictions

Many addicts may be able to stop drinking or taking drugs but turn instead to other compulsive behaviors such as workaholism, caffeine ingestion or foodaholism in an attempt to "white-knuckle it." These cross-addictions mask the root and reinforce denial.

3. Blame-laying

Perfectionism renders the addict incapable of taking responsibility for wrongs done to himself or others as a result of his addiction. Blaming others for one's addiction and problems becomes a habit that also reinforces denial.

4. Impulsive decision-making

The addict's raw emotions fueled by hidden anger usually move him to make sudden life-controlling decisions, such as job changes, taking a marriage partner and making financial decisions that affect his future. These often complicate recovery and add stress to his life.

5. Repetitive backsliding

If a Christian is prone to backsliding, it is possible he has a drug or alcohol history or other addiction such as gambling or sexual addiction. In the face of addictive cravings, he will tend to forget the bad effects he has suffered and offer weak excuses for returning to addictions. Rather than simply choosing to leave the Lord and the Church, an addict runs away in shame using a mask of bravado to hide his sense of failure. During the denial phase of the addictive cycle, he usually returns to church thinking all is well—until next time.

6. *Anger*

Addicts are usually incapable of dealing appropriately with anger. Many have a rage they have handled with the use of an addictive substance or action. This anger vents itself on others (in the form of argumentativeness, verbal and physical abuse) or on themselves (in the form of depression). Christian addicts tend to get angry with God and the Church when things go wrong. In chapter 13, we will examine the many faces of hidden anger and learn God's solution for recognizing it and releasing it appropriately.

7. *Religious perfectionism*

Addicts who turn to the Church during the denial phase of addiction may have real spiritual experiences, but they often develop a self-righteous religious mask, making it difficult to admit true faults. Religious addiction, whereby the addict involves himself in the addictive cycle using extreme "religious" disciplines and forms of self-martyrdom as his mood-alterer, is a dangerous substitute addiction. We will be looking at these issues and the way out of the bondage of religious perfectionism in chapter 14.

8. *Rebelliousness*

The self-righteous mask and religious perfectionism usually manifest themselves in the Church as rebellion against the pastor, elders, deacons or established guidelines. Rigid in their approach to life, such rebels tend to be legalistic and unteachable in biblical interpretation and in their expectations of others in the church. Conformity is difficult for them, and they frequently circumvent it and establish, as did the

Pharisees of Jesus' day, their own brand of righteousness. On the job, they may rebel against the office manager or the CEO.

9. *Compulsive talking*

Many addicts who are trying to live without their substances and processes become compulsive talkers, rattling on nonstop out of nervousness. This trait also manifests itself in the form of dominating conversations and group discussions as well as compulsive phone-calling.

10. *Lying*

Gamblers Anonymous has a joke: "How can you tell when a compulsive gambler is lying? When you see his lips move." Denial of addiction has become a way of life with the addict, which results in an inability to perceive reality accurately. To hide symptoms of addiction, he resorts to lying, which becomes a habit sustained out of fear. Lying becomes such a habit for an addict that even when he is not indulging in his addiction, he continues to exaggerate and tell "white" lies as an automatic learned response to uneasy feelings.

11. *Secrecy*

Beware if an addict begins to cloak his activities and whereabouts in secrecy. Attempting to hide addiction reinforces denial and prevents discovery and intervention. Even when not reverting to the addictive behavior, many addicts resort to living in secrecy and studiously avoid living open lives.

12. Control

Addicts attempt to dominate their circumstances to ensure the availability of their mood-alterers and to protect themselves from vulnerability. This often manifests itself in the desire to grab center stage in the congregation, to stir up crises, to rise to positions of leadership quickly or to control the circumstances around them by controlling others. Many want influence and authority without the accompanying responsibilities.

13. Self-pity

Out of the belief that no one truly cares about him rises the addict's tendency toward self-pity when a situation gets too big for him to handle. Feeling sorry for himself gives the addict an excuse to indulge himself in his addictive substance. An addict in a church sometimes feels sorry for himself in order to draw the attention of the pastor or other church members. If his emotional temper tantrums do not attract the desired response, he advances, sometimes subtly, to the point of threatening to leave and sometimes carrying out his threats. The worst thing the rest of the congregation can do is chase after him. The result would be an emotional tug-of-war.

Healing Is a Process: Why Did Jack Fail?

What happened to Jack, the alcoholic who finally left the church? Was he really born again in the first place?

Yes, he was saved. He was born again and received a new spirit the moment he asked God to forgive him and Jesus Christ to save him.

Jack's inconsistent behavior was a result of a conflict of two voices in his internal monologue. One was the voice of his old flesh and the other the voice of his new spirit. Jack's problems were complicated by the return of the addictive cycle. His mind needed the gradual renewing of the Holy Spirit as well as physical healing and restoration, a process that ordinarily takes years. Because Jack was convinced that healing was always an "event" rather than a "process," he believed his spiritual experiences had furnished him with the single dose of God necessary to produce all he needed. He claimed the verses "I'm a new creation. . . . Old things are passed away, all things have become new. . ." and "Forgetting what lies behind . . . ," but his emotions had not yet caught up with his spiritual experiences, a process that is accomplished only through the gradual renewing of the mind on a daily basis.

What Could Jack's Church Have Done?

Jack's friends were right when they encouraged him to face his addiction by going to A.A. Unless addiction is addressed directly, the addict will either return to his addiction, become cross-addicted or become impossible to live with. The Church must learn to heed the warning of the apostle Paul concerning the appointment of addicts to leadership. The new believer must be given a period of years for his emotions to catch up to his spirit, to sit at the feet of Jesus and the ministries of the Church and "learn of Him," and time for his addiction to be subdued. He must be tested in his response to authority and given a chance to learn to apply the Gospel at home, to learn to weather crises by the application of biblical principles. Because Jack was appointed to a leadership role before these things were worked into his character, he became "conceited and [fell] into the condemnation incurred by the devil" (see 1 Timothy 3:6).

What Should Jack Do Now?

If you are "Jack," you need to humble yourself in the face of your addiction and confess to your Christian friends your need for help. Whenever you realize that your craving is returning, that is the time to seek help from counseling. Perhaps you feel that it is too late, that you have already caused so much damage that you can never recover the lost friendships you severed as a result of your addiction. For some of those friendships it may be too late, but for your conscience's sake, get into treatment and attempt to reestablish them on a firm foundation of honesty and repentance. It is never too late for that, and you may be surprised to see God's grace miraculously and gradually heal those impossible situations.

What Should Teresa Do Now?

Jack made the mistake of taking on too much responsibility too soon. As every addict in treatment needs to do, Jack should have given his family time to adjust to the "new" husband and father. Addicts typically feel they have changed and expect others to understand and adjust immediately. The fragile emotions of Jack's family, wounded by his addiction, needed time to heal before healthy family relationships could be established.

Jack's return to drinking was not Teresa's fault. No matter what she or anyone close to Jack did, he was headed for relapse unless he sought help. If you are "Teresa," you should now continue to be faithful to your local church, open yourself to an understanding Christian friend—of the same sex—for prayer and sharing, seek counseling from your pastor as needed and begin attending a support group for families in your situation, such as Al-Anon or Adult Children of Alcoholics, if the problem is alcohol. You should explore the possibility of conducting an intervention, which we will discuss in just a minute. Your children also need to understand that their father's addiction is not their fault and they should be encouraged to attend a support group, too. In no case should you accept responsibility for Jack's addiction. The same God who saved him can deliver him.

If Teresa and her boys fail to get help, they will likely become "addicted to an addict," an emotional condition known as co-dependency. This form of addiction affects many in the Church who do not recognize the symptoms affecting their behavior and the happiness of their Christian lives.

In the following chapter, we will discuss this all-consuming addiction, but first I want to suggest a way to help a loved one face his problem.

Getting Help for Others

The last of the Twelve Steps reads, "Having had a spiritual awakening as a result of these steps, we tried to carry this message to others, and to practice these principles in all our affairs." Part of carrying the message of addiction recovery to others involves protecting your family members and friends from the deceptive destruction of addiction. While you cannot assume responsibility for the actions and for the recovery of others, it is up to you to speak to those you love if you see a life-threatening addiction creeping into their lives. If you are a family member, driving out the giants in the land means alerting others to the danger of addiction. Speaking to others about their bondage is not easy and takes much courage, but the Scripture admonishes us, "Brethren, even if a man is caught in any trespass, you who are spiritual, restore such a one in a spirit of gentleness; looking to yourselves, lest you too be tempted" (Galatians 6:1). Because you have been through it and have taken the beam out of your own eye, you can now see clearly to help your brother remove the splinter from his and begin to recover.

In speaking to a family member or a close friend about his addiction, find a time when you are alone and begin to tell him in a gentle tone of voice what you see happening to him and briefly share with him your story. An addict in denial may not respond to this form of confrontation by seeking help, but give it a try anyway. His life is at stake. If he doesn't take your advice, don't give up. Take another recovering addict with you and talk to him about it again. If he still refuses to recognize a problem or carry through with treatment, you may need to conduct what is known as an "intervention." An intervention is a planned meeting attended by close relatives and friends, not previously announced to the addict, in which the addict is confronted about the harm his addiction is causing himself and others around him. Many recovering addicts were brought into treatment after an intervention had shaken them to the emotional core.

A properly conducted intervention surprises the addict, disarms him and allows each member to describe the hurt the addict has caused because of the addiction. It is a demonstration of "tough love," and is often met by tears, anger, manipulation, blame-laying and denial on the part of the addict.

But God never promised that driving out the giants would be easy.

Before collecting the family and confronting the addict, it is wise to seek professional counseling for the family about how to conduct an intervention so that there is a display of unity toward the addict rather than division. Sometimes the addict's employer is allowed to be present to describe the effects his addiction has had on his job performance. This helps the addict decide to seek help immediately. When he sees that he can have a leave of absence from his job, he has no other excuse and may submit more willingly.

Have the car keys in hand, his bag packed and a reservation made at a treatment center so that the addict can be transported immediately to treatment before he has a chance to compose himself and reinforce denial. Mary Ellen Pinkham, best-selling author, wrote in her book *How to Stop the One You Love From Drinking* about an intervention a friend tried on her that didn't work. The friend left the room to make a phone call, leaving Mary Ellen time to compose herself. "In the end, I convinced myself that between one thing and another, there was no way I could be tied up by checking into a center. (As a matter of fact, I decided I'd have to be tied up if anyone wanted to get me into a center.)"

If an intervention doesn't work, keep trying. Confront as often as it takes to get an addict into treatment—but plan each one and don't try it alone. If the addict refuses treatment, it may be necessary to detach yourself from him emotionally so that his "leaven" doesn't spread to the other members of the family. If physical or sexual abuse is involved, he is violating the law and legal action should be taken. You may be jeopardizing yourself legally as well as morally to cover up for him. Consult an attorney, your pastor and a sympathetic counselor for advice before making any life-controlling decisions. Only you can make the decision that is right for you. But realize that Jesus does not expect you to live life as a victim. He will either give you the grace to walk through the situation unscathed, physically, emotionally and spiritually, or lead you on a pathway out of danger.

8
People Addiction: The Counterfeit Agape

Living in the presence of glaring human need creates the perfect setting for one of the most common and unnoticed forms of addiction—the addiction to people.

The term *addiction to people* or *people addict* seems contrary to the teaching of Christ, who commands us to love one another by laying down our lives for the brethren. One has only to read the Gospels to see Jesus Christ totally consumed with others.

Or was He? The truth is that Jesus was not consumed with the need to sacrifice Himself for others, but to do the will of His Father. At times that involved laying His own interests aside, but it was out of obedience—not sacrifice for the sake of finding His identity. The Body of Christ is filled with people, like Claudia, who do not know the line between obedience and sacrifice.

Claudia

Claudia had come to Jesus Christ the week after she had married Ned, a drug dealer and an addict who had dabbled in occultism. Claudia's sparkling green eyes and pink cheeks framed a compassionate smile and projected an innocence and eagerness for all God had to offer. Unable to see her father's "drinking problem" as alcoholism, and unaware of the family patterns that result from alcoholism, Claudia had learned to be a patient wife from watching her mother endure heartache. She was able, like her mother, to take abuse like a soldier and rise above the situation even before she became a Christian.

To complicate matters, the teaching at Claudia's church encouraged submission to her husband regardless of the stormy circumstances, so Claudia immersed herself in trying to lay her own life down for Ned in the belief that, because of her obedience, one day he would come to his senses. This dream of the Christian home they would have someday kept Claudia in very dark times.

The phone at Claudia's pastor's home rang often as she called for prayer and talked openly with the pastor's wife about her troubles. Four years went by during which Claudia was shoved against the wall on various occasions, forced to perform sexual acts with her husband that she felt were indecent, and cover for her husband's drug business. The lilt of joy once in her voice faded to the sigh of martyrdom and sacrifice. Because of the emphasis on submission at her church, Claudia shut off all thoughts that God would allow her to step out of the situation. Her Christian friends prayed with her and consoled her, but never offered her any hint that God was anything but honored by her decision to stay with Ned.

One night Ned slipped up behind Claudia, grabbed her around the neck and began to choke her. Just when she felt she would never draw another breath, Ned let her go, laughing as though he derived an eerie pleasure out of pretending to kill her. Claudia was sure that when the Lord took charge of his life, these things would go.

When Claudia gave birth to a baby girl, Clara, taking care of her was the only joy in Claudia's life. One night, in a fit of rage, Ned dragged the baby's dirty diapers out of the pail, smeared the excrement on the walls and stormed out of the house leaving Claudia to clean up while he took the baby with him for a walk in the nearby woods.

Several hours passed. Claudia paced the floor, marshaling the forces of prayer. When the door finally opened, her husband floated through the door, "stoned," but carrying the baby. But as Claudia laid Clara in the crib, she noticed small round burns on her baby's body. After Ned left the house, she reached for the phone, but instead of dialing her own pastor, she phoned another pastor in the same city.

I will leave to wiser heads the theological issues of divorce in such a situation. But *separation* is another matter. I have no hesitation—and we teach this in our church—that in these extreme cases when a person is abused, as were Claudia and her baby, the remedy is to break the relationship, at least temporarily.

In Claudia's case, that is what happened. She left Ned when under counseling she came to realize that she had become a people addict.

What Is the Christian People Addict?

If you are a Christian people addict, you are the pastor whose sense of self-worth is inextricably tied to his ministry, the elderly woman who sends her life savings to an unprincipled television evangelist, the churchgoer who compromises his beliefs to remain loyal to a lifeless church, the Christian who seeks to please people more than God. The Christian people addict derives his sense of worth from sacrificing himself for people when God has never told him to do so.

As much as an alcoholic turns to the bottle and a drug addict turns to drugs, the people addict, co-dependent or "savior" turns to absorbing himself with unhappy people in the hope of sacrificing for their benefit. He somehow feels, even though he would never say so, that the unhappy person's well-being hangs on his ability to protect him. He cleans up after him, takes responsibility for his sorrows, actually helps the "problem person" lie to himself.

The unhappy outcome is that in so doing, rather than rescuing the person, the "savior" is actually keeping him from facing his problem and turning to the real Savior for help. Rather than keeping Jesus Christ at the center of his life, the co-dependent is ruled by the "problem person." Gradually, the "problem person" consumes more and more of his time until the co-dependent's life is molded around him, obsessed with him.

With all this "holy" preoccupation it would seem that the people addict would be full of joy, but the opposite is true. The people addict's emotional state is a vacuum. Because he lives in a symbiotic relationship with crises, he winds up climbing onto a roller coaster with the "problem person." In order to prevent further hurt he shuts down his emotions. He becomes driven by a sense of obligation and duty, "giving his body to be burned" (1 Corinthians 13:3) without the sense of joy and peace that comes from true obedience to the Lord Jesus Christ.

The people addict maintains a smile on his face, but his eyes are filled with pain. He has swallowed anger and frustration so often that he is filled with resentment: His sacrifices have not produced real, lasting change in the "problem person." Without realizing it, he has extended himself into a situation that God has not given him the grace to handle. He becomes angry with the person for not changing and angry with God for not forcing His hand against the will of the "problem person."

Such was the case with the Brooks family, a wife and six children all developing into people addicts around Mr. Brooks, a verbal abuser. Because the Brooks attended their church faithfully, the pastor and choir members could tell when Mr. Brooks was in a good mood because his family seated beside him had pleasant expressions on their faces. But when Mr. Brooks had been, like the abusive King Saul, "raving in the midst of his house," it was written on the faces of his family. The smiles were erased and instead their faces bore the tired, pained expressions of disillusionment, the results of his wounding words. The power of death was in his tongue and served to impart the same gloomy expression on his face to those in his family. Here is how such a people addiction develops.

The Development of People Addiction

The progression into people addiction is depicted in the following series of drawings:

Figure 1. In the first stage of addiction, the potential people addict (at right) is reasonably happy but emotionally vul-

nerable, longing for a relationship that he believes will fill an emotional void. The "problem person" (center) is unhappy because his life is ruled by Satan (left) who has led him captive to do his, Satan's, will.

Figure 2. The vulnerable person attaches himself to the "problem person." He is at first unaware that indirectly he, too, has attached himself to Satan. No unpleasant demands have been made on the relationship, and the codependent seems perfectly happy to have found someone to rescue.

Figure 3. The vulnerable person begins to suffer under the emotional chains that bind him to the unhealthy, unhappy person. Demands begin to be made on the relationship, demands that strain the vulnerable person. He becomes manipulated and controlled because he is afraid to assert himself for fear of what the unhappy person might do. He often fears loneliness more than the unhealthy relationship.

Figure 4. As the "problem person" continues to make demands on the relationship, demanding more sacrifice and more attention, the face of the co-dependent begins to look as miserable as that of the unhealthy person to whom he has attached himself. The people addict is now aware that he is controlled, in bondage to that person, but feels unable to break himself free.

Figure 5. By separating from the unhealthy relationship, the people addict reasserts the Lordship of Jesus Christ in his life, which had been temporarily replaced with devotion to the unhappy, Satan-controlled individual. The people addict once again begins to experience peace and happiness.

101

Figure 6. Rather than leave himself emotionally vulnerable to a similar experience, the people addict attaches himself to Jesus Christ instead, determining to be led by the Holy Spirit into relationships rather than by the lusts and desires of his flesh, no matter how noble they may seem.

Testing Relationships

After learning about people addiction, you may be wondering if you are involved in an unhealthy relationship. The following quiz should help you answer questions about a relationship that may be addictive. Answer the following questions:

_____ 1. Is the person I am trying to help an addict, the son or daughter of an addict or emotionally abusive person, or does he/she have a stagnant problem, one that is always there and never changes?

_____ 2. Does he/she *follow* sound counsel and advice or ignore it?

_____ 3. Does he/she demand more and more attention as the relationship progresses?

_____ 4. Has the Lord truly assured me that my efforts on his/her behalf will be redemptive?

_____ 5. Do I have to compromise my beliefs to stand by him/her?

_____ 6. Am I the only one giving in the relationship? Is the giving clearly out of balance?

_____ 7. Does the time spent with this person interfere with my devotion to the Lord, to other priority relationships, my job or my church attendance?

_____ 8. Are my conversations with this person almost always centered around his/her needs?

_____ 9. Have I been emotionally, physically or financially abused by this person?

_____10. Do I feel joy when I hear his/her voice on the other end of the phone?

_____11. Do I often entangle myself in relationships in which I rescue and manage the lives of others?

_____12. Is the good I am able to do for him/her beginning to be outweighed by the harm he/she is doing to me?

_____13. Am I afraid to break the relationship for fear of hurting him/her, being lonely myself or because I am afraid of what he/she may do to him/herself, others or me?

_____14. Am I jeopardizing myself legally to cover up his/her activities?

_____15. Did I grow up in a dysfunctional home myself?

_____16. Am I becoming a "crutch" for him/her, preventing him/her from learning to find out God's will on his/her own, thus actually standing between him/her and God?

Score: Again, no quiz is definitive, but this one can perhaps help you see a troubling relationship in a new light. The following answers indicate people addiction: *No* to numbers 4 and 10, *ignore* to number 2, and *yes* to the others. If you answered four questions with these responses, take a long look at the relationship. If you answered more than five with these responses, the relationship is very likely addictive. You probably should consider getting addiction counseling or joining a support group. If abuse is present, you especially need guidance. You are not helping a person by letting him hurt you—physically or emotionally. The enemy will use him to destroy you and the person both.

The Spiritual Effects of People Addiction

The spiritual condition of the people addict is tragic. All his energy has been poured into "rescuing the perishing and caring for the dying" so that he has no time to sit at the feet of Jesus, look after his personal needs or the needs of other family members and friends. The patron saint of the people addict is Martha, the sister of Mary, who when faced with a visit from Jesus flew into a flurry of activity and absorbed herself in giving, leaving herself no time to be with Jesus. She was offering sacrifices that Jesus never asked for, expecting her sister to help shoulder the burden, and won, not Jesus' praise, but His gentle reproof: "Martha, Martha, you are worried and bothered about so many things; but only a few things are necessary, really only one, for Mary has chosen the good part, which shall not be taken away from her" (Luke 10:41–42). In effect Jesus told her, "I am not going to order Mary to get up and help you, because you are out of God's will with all this extraneous sacrifice."

The people addict has reordered the second commandment

of Jesus Christ, "Love your neighbor," to be the first, and has changed it to, "Thou shalt love your neighbor *instead of* yourself." He has redefined *agape* and substituted a counterfeit. To the people addict, love is martyrdom with little hope of present reward or visible fruit.

Where Do People Addicts Come From?

People addicts are not born; they are formed by the environment in which they were nurtured as children. The presence of a major dysfunction, such as an addiction, a handicap or some other source of shame, causes the attention to be focused directly or subconsciously on the "problem person." Claudia (married to Ned) was born into an alcoholic home, one where addiction was present and covered over by the members of the family. As a result, the home of Claudia's parents operated by the same laws as do other dysfunctional homes, the laws outlined by Wayne Kritsberg in *The Adult Children of Alcoholics Syndrome:* denial, silence, rigidity and isolation. These laws rule the unhealthy home because of the presence of four specific underlying fears that prevent healthy relationships.

1. The Fear of the Truth

Those in a dysfunctional home are afraid to admit the presence of addiction and will go to great lengths to deny the fact that any extraordinary problem exists. As we will discuss in a later chapter, denial exists in the addict and the lie is perpetuated by the other members of the family.

2. *The Fear of Communicating*

The members of a dysfunctional family are afraid to talk about the addiction and other problems openly. Instead, euphemisms, gestures and other family signals are used to denote "the problem," such as using the term *drinking problem* instead of *alcoholism*. Because the family rules do not permit disclosure of the problem, the members must also squelch the anger and frustration that surround it. The children grow up seeing the problem, but not being able to talk about it. As a result, their communication skills become impaired and carry over into their future relationships.

3. *The Fear of Change*

As miserable as the atmosphere may seem in a dysfunctional home, the members actually prefer the status quo to any change—even a good one. If one member changes, all members must adjust. In order to prevent change, family members work overtime to control situations and people. The children grow up rigid in their actions and beliefs, fearing deviation from any established circumstances and conditions.

4. *The Fear of Fellowship*

The dysfunctional home becomes isolated from other families in the community. In order to keep the family's secret, the family refuses to fellowship with others and prefers to be a self-sufficient entity. Fellowship with others would bring change; therefore, the dysfunctional family either moves about frequently, interrupting any relationships that might develop, or keeps to itself on the block. In the church, people who were reared in dysfunctional homes tend to keep their home lives completely private, some remaining on the fringes of the congregation while others busy themselves in activities to substitute for the development of meaningful relationships.

The presence of these fears and their resulting laws promote a stagnant situation that exists sometimes for decades without any movement or significant change. In Claudia's case, two of her brothers became alcoholics and all the children married addicts and abusive people who were used to operating by the same unwritten laws.

The Roles

When a family operates according to the binding fears enumerated above, the family members take on roles peculiar but standard to all dysfunctional homes.* These roles have become widely accepted as essential to the diagnosis and treatment of families who live in the presence of addiction. Each role defines a distinct form of people addiction.

The Hero in the dysfunctional home diverts attention from the problem person by excelling. He is the valedictorian, the member of Who's Who, the gridiron hero. He is perfectionistic in his expectations of himself because, subconsciously, the hero takes the responsibility of proving the family's worth to the rest of the world.

The Clown covers his emotional pain and breaks the tension felt in the dysfunctional home with humor and laughter. He serves as a mascot for the home and rallies the members by keeping them joking about the situations, refocusing attention from the addict and onto the humor of the moment.

---

* These roles were first set forth in *Another Chance: Hope and Health for the Alcoholic Family* by Sharon Wegscheider-Cruse.

The Placater spends his time moving from person to person, making sure each family member's feelings are not hurt. He often serves as a diplomat, carrying messages from one family member to another so they will not have to communicate directly with each other. He will compromise, cajole and soothe by any means necessary to keep emotional displays at a minimum. He cannot stand to see people cry or shout.

The Scapegoat refocuses attention from the addict in the family by getting involved in trouble himself. He may become addicted or resort to illegal or immoral practices to cover his emotional pain. As the scapegoat in the Old Testament carried the sins of the camp of Israel into the desert, so the family scapegoat seeks to make himself "more sinful" than the addict who originally generated the family's dysfunction.

The Lost Child fades into the wallpaper, hiding in his own world of fantasy. This member of the family makes average grades, never distinguishes himself, rarely opens his mouth to offer his opinions or interact with the family and draws attention to himself by his silence. He grows up prone to depression and introspection, insecure and unsure of himself in other relationships.

While a family member usually assumes a role and keeps it for life, sometimes family members cross roles or assume more than one. When a member of a dysfunctional family comes to Jesus Christ, God will, through the renewing of his mind, begin to heal him of people addiction. If the person does not allow the Lord to change him, he will inevitably retain the fears, operate by the same laws and maintain the roles for life, carrying them over into his Christian family and church. Instead of functioning as a healthy member of the Body of Christ, he will function instead as a hurting, dysfunctional member, often isolating himself and finding the development of healthy relationships difficult. If it is true that some eighty percent of our churches are filled with adults and children from dysfunctional homes, it is little wonder that church-hopping, mistrust and broken relationships abound in the Body of Christ.

What About Claudia?

Should Claudia have stepped out of her relationship with Ned? I believe so. Never was Claudia given any suggestion that Ned would change. When he became physically and sex-ually abusive and persisted in illegal, drug-related activities, Claudia was legally and physically jeopardizing herself and her baby daughter by remaining with him. As Christians we are not to "participate in the unfruitful deeds of darkness, but instead even expose them," as Paul told the Ephesians (5:11). In his heart and with his actions, Ned had actually "left" Claudia, even though his clothes were still in the closet. He turned on her with a vengeance, unwilling to tolerate her life as a Christian.

Claudia made the same mistake many other well-meaning Christians make. She believed that the Scriptures teach it was up to her to effect change in her husband. Thus, she took over the role as "savior" from the Lord Jesus Christ. When Ned never changed, but only became harder and more dan-gerous to live with, Claudia felt she had failed. This was complicated by the attitudes of her Christian friends who were quick to tell her she would sin if she left her husband. In attempting to win him to Christ, however, she almost defiled herself. The Law of Moses illustrates the mistake Claudia made, which all but succeeded in luring her away from Jesus Christ.

A Lesson from the Mosaic Law

The Old Testament priest in Israel was not permitted to observe the funeral customs as other Hebrews were allowed to do. God spoke specifically about this: "The priest . . . shall not . . . approach any dead person, nor defile himself even for his father or his mother" (Leviticus 21:10–11). In grieving for their loved ones, the Hebrews often cut themselves, shaved their heads and flung themselves wailing over the dead bodies. But not the priests. For them to do so would bring spiritual defilement and interrupt their ability to offer sacrifices and stand in the presence of the Lord. This has great meaning when we realize that Christians are called to serve God as priests.

And yet remember that Jesus, the great High Priest, did touch the dead in obedience to His Father. Does that seem like a contradiction? On one occasion, for instance, Jesus stopped the funeral procession of a poor widow's only son. To the horror of His disciples, the Son of God reached out and touched the coffin. Had he defiled Himself, He would have been disqualified from making the atonement. But here is the distinction. To everyone's amazement, the dead man sat up and began to speak. So it is when Jesus touches not only the physically dead, but the spiritually dead. Rather than defiling Himself for a dead person, the life-giving Spirit of God intervenes.

And so it is when we touch the lives of the spiritually dead in obedience to the Lord. They rise and offer us no threat of defilement. If we linger over the spiritually dead, however, fling ourselves across their carcasses, damaging ourselves on their behalf when God has not instructed us to do so, we become defiled ourselves and risk sacrificing our own fellowship with God. This is what was happening with Claudia and countless other Christians who are in danger of sacrificing themselves for "dead" persons out of misunderstanding the will of God.

What Claudia did not realize was that the type of love she had was a counterfeit for true Christian *agape* love. It became a replacement for real consecration and set her up for spiritual burnout. When we realize the end of counterfeit love, it is easy to recognize its source as satanic. The counterfeit *agape* works the works of the devil whose purposes are "to steal, and kill, and destroy" (John 10:10).

What is the solution? If you are a people addict, like any other addict, you must sever yourself from the source of your addiction in order to be healed. Like the father in the parable Jesus told of the Prodigal Son, you must muster true *agape* love (which sets limits for yourself and others for whom you are responsible) and care enough to correct and be able to release "problem people," allowing God to do His work in their lives.

People addiction is a counterfeit for true Christian love. Its design is to become a substitute for the real and prevent you and the person you are too attached to from experiencing genuine love. The real *agape* love and the ways of developing and maintaining healthy relationships will be discussed in chapter 16.

As in the case of people addiction, every other addiction is also a substitute for the real byproducts of the Holy Spirit's presence in our lives. But how do we break addiction's cruel hold? Is it a disease or a sin? Who is to blame? Where does addiction lead? In the following chapter, we will discover the major hindrance to overcoming an addiction and how to break that hindrance.

9
"I Can't Be an Addict—I'm a Christian"

She can't be an alcoholic; she's my wife! proclaimed a billboard advertising a treatment center near Pittsburgh. Another one reads, *Mom can't be an addict; her doctor gave her the pills!* These statements are common exclamations family members make when confronted with the fact that their loved ones are addicts.

But what about when the addict is someone you love? Have you heard things like these lately? "I'm not an alcoholic; I haven't had a drink in months!" "I'm overweight, but I'm not a food addict." "I'm not an addict; I can stop when I want to." "I'm not an addict; I'm a child of God."

If you have heard—or even said—things like these you are not alone. Some famous people are with you. One outstanding example was baseball star Pete Rose who said, on the day he was banned from major league baseball for betting on the game, "I don't have a problem with gambling and, therefore, I won't be seeking help of any kind. . . ."

It was Jesus Christ who said, "The mouth speaks out of that which fills the heart" (Matthew 12:34). Statements like those just quoted are spoken out of the hearts of people who are caught in a realm of deception known as *denial*, the inability to perceive one's true condition—spiritually, emotionally or physically—in relation to addiction.

All forms of denial, though, are not necessarily bad. In the presence of an extreme emotional or physical shock, human emotions sometimes cease to function temporarily. Lasting a few moments, a few hours or a few weeks, denial can move a person through what would otherwise cause an emotional breakdown. When a loved one dies or an accident occurs, it is the phenomenon of denial that cushions the shock so that the human being can continue to function. Usually denial does not last, but subsides as the person comes to realize and accept the truth gradually. This form of denial is useful to the human being in times of emergency. But denial can all too easily be used to cover unpleasant realities, things like sins, life-threatening diseases and our old enemy, addiction.

Addiction gathers strength from denial. And denial gathers its strength from fear—the fear of facing a reality with which someone believes he cannot cope or that he does not wish to change. Denial not only prevents a person from perceiving reality but enables him to substitute a false or incomplete concept of reality in its place.

A Mother's "Love"

Everyone who knew Carolyn Baker well knew that she was living in denial. Carolyn's husband divorced her after seventeen years of marriage, leaving her to raise three teenagers alone. The two older children, Jennifer and Bob, were model students and a joy to her. They helped their mother maintain a semblance of family unity in the face of gaping emotional wounds.

The problem came with Teddy, the youngest. Teddy was a loner, spending a lot of time in his room. He had few friends and led a private existence. When Teddy entered middle school he became moody and depressed at times. His grades dropped abruptly. He was often afflicted with a runny nose and red eyes that made his mother think he had contracted some kind of allergy.

As the months wore on, Bob and Jennifer began to hear that their brother was involved with the wrong crowd. When Carolyn heard about it, she reassured Bob and Jennifer that Teddy had been brought up the same way they had, and that he knew how to say no. Then things began to disappear from the house, things like an heirloom brooch and Jennifer's stereo. Bob and Jennifer had begun to notice that the things were missing after Teddy and his friends had left the house, but Carolyn insisted that they were misplaced or borrowed. Once when Teddy was confronted, he flew into an angry rage, slamming the door of his room so hard that the dishes rattled. Wanting to believe that Teddy was a victim of circumstances, Carolyn tried her best to pretend that things were normal, believing that, in time, Teddy would "outgrow this stage."

One night after Carolyn was in bed, the phone rang. It was the police. They had arrested Teddy and booked him for cocaine possession. But even as the police officer was speaking, Carolyn was arguing mentally that it wasn't really Teddy but his friends who had done wrong.

It wasn't until Carolyn was talking with one of her friends from her Bible study group that she came crashing out of her fantasy world. "Carolyn," her friend told her, " Teddy is an addict and everyone in town knows it but you!" The truth was that Carolyn really had known it all along. She feared the exposure of the awful truth that gnawed at her constantly. Guilt-ridden for not being "a good mother," Carolyn ignored the warning signs of beginning drug addiction in Teddy to protect her own emotions and her reputation. She had fallen into the people addict's trap, covering for her loved one through a strange mixture of her brand of love and selfishness, perpetuated by her denial to herself and others that the problem existed.

Why would a Christian woman like Carolyn do such a thing? Where does denial come from?

What Began It All

Denial was first practiced by Adam and Eve after having tasted fruit from the one tree God declared off-limits to them. As soon as they sinned, their eyes were opened and they saw the nakedness of their flesh.

Gripped with fear and embarrassment, they reached out for the leaves adorning a nearby fig bush. In a pitiful attempt to cover the reality of their nakedness, they stitched fig leaves together to make garments for themselves. They were still hiding in the bushes when God came for His daily appointment with them.

Anyone who is hiding an addiction is "wearing fig leaves" and is under the mysterious spell of the law of denial. In order to enter recovery, he must identify this law of denial and break it. It may not be as easy as it sounds, but as we explore the following fig leaves of denial, we will learn to recognize it.

Fig Leaf 1: Fear of Facing the Truth

Since Eden, man has been afraid of the truth. We are afraid that the truth will present us with a reality so harsh that we cannot overcome it. So we hide as Adam and Eve hid from God. The feeling that we are inadequate to meet the challenge of truth leaves us naked, so we reach out for the fig leaf of denial.

Fig Leaf 2: Ignoring the Problem

One way to keep from finding answers to a problem is to pretend the problem doesn't exist. Ignoring symptoms can postpone the trauma of facing facts. An addict will go to great lengths to ignore the problem. Someone who is co-dependent, for instance, will help a "problem person" by entering into his fantasy world and pretending with him or by keeping him from facing the negative consequences of his addiction.

If the addict is a binge-er, able to maintain himself without indulging for periods of time, he may begin to feel he is in control. Addicts need to remember that they are not addicts because they *feel* like it, but because they follow the addictive cycle.

Fig Leaf 3: Minimization

One day the addict may give in to what others are saying and begin to admit he has a problem. The fig leaf of minimization, however, accommodates denial by preventing him from associating his behavior with addictive patterns or his actions with destructive consequences. He will use euphemisms and understatements to keep from recognizing the acuteness of the problem. *Pleasingly plump* instead of *fat*, *drinking problem* instead of *alcoholism*, *bad habit* instead of *addiction* are a few popular minimizations.

Fig Leaf 4: Rationalization

When minimization crumbles, rationalization is quick to replace it. This means justifying actions. "I deserve to get high because. . . ." Self-pity is the stem on which the fig leaf of rationalization grows. Addicts develop elaborate cases for maintaining their behavior. They blame family members for problems and addictions. "If you were a decent wife, I wouldn't have to drink. . . ."

Fig Leaf 5: Procrastination

"I'll think about that tomorrow," was Scarlett O'Hara's famous reaction in *Gone with the Wind*. It gave her a way to cope with guilt: simply put off thinking about it. Someone once said, "The road to hell is paved with good intentions." The fig leaf of procrastination sometimes remains when all the others have slipped; it can stall addiction recovery for years.

Fig Leaf 6: Humor

Making light of the problem, joking about impending disaster, is an unusually effective form of denial: "If I eat anything, I'm going to die! Ha! Ha! Ha! So I might as well indulge!" It is the companion of rationalization. Laughing about the problem breaks the tension and fends off conviction. But doesn't it sound a little like the rich fool in Jesus' parable: "Soul, . . . take your ease, eat, drink and be merry" (Luke 12:19)?

Fig Leaf 7: Misapplying Scriptures

We Christians are great at this one! In order to barricade ourselves against the nudging of the Holy Spirit, we simply reapply a few Scriptures to cover the naked truth: "Forgetting what lies behind . . ." "There is no condemnation for those who are in Christ Jesus . . ." or "If any man is in Christ, he is a new creature: the old things have passed away; behold, new things have come." We don't try on *these* Scriptures: "He who conceals his transgressions will not prosper" (Proverbs 28:13) or "Having these promises, beloved, let us cleanse ourselves from all defilement of flesh and spirit, perfecting holiness in the fear of God" (2 Corinthians 7:1). Satan tried taking Scriptures out of context in tempting Jesus Christ. It's far better to face the truth than risk lifelong addiction and early death.

Fig Leaf 8: False Positive Thinking and Confession

The soul attempting to reassure itself that everything is fine is an elaborate fig leaf. Grabbing at religious phrases and applying them to oneself to escape the truth is the soul's attempt to recover from the Fall by itself. Positivism *when it does not proceed out of the gentle voice of the Holy Spirit* profits nothing. Trying to convince ourselves that negative facts do not exist because we are Christian is a form of denial masquerading as a Christian doctrine. True faith does not deny reality but walks through it. The apostle Paul wrote, "His strength is perfected in my weakness, for when I am weak, then am I strong" (2 Corinthians 12:9–10). Today's Christian usually says, "What weakness? I have the power to rule and reign!"

118

Fig Leaf 9: Lack of Discernment

The inability to recognize the difference between the work of the Holy Spirit and the works of the flesh reinforces denial. Addictive patterns and behavior tend to disguise themselves as "spiritual boldness" or "faith" or "dedication." This is especially true of people addicts who seem to be patient when in fact they are filled with anger and depression.

Another manifestation of this fig leaf is the inability to discern the origin of guilt. Is it coming from the devil or from the conviction of the Holy Spirit? Often when the Spirit of God helps us see truth, we condemn Him as being the voice of the devil.

Fig Leaf 10: False Guilt

An addict tends to use the hopeless feeling of having sinned against God and others to fling himself farther away from recovery and deeper into addiction. Hopeless guilt comes from the devil who assures him he is guilty of a terrible crime; there is no hope. Many addicts deny that help exists and is available to them. This belief is reinforced whenever the addict attempts to reassert his willpower to deal with the addiction and fails miserably, going back to his addictive substance or process. Because he fails to meet a standard he has set for himself, he feels guilty.

In *Willpower's Not Enough,* Arnold Washton and Donna Boundy explain, "The belief that an addict is a 'bad person' perpetuates the problem. That's why it's so important to reframe addiction in a nonjudgmental light, to separate who you are from the addiction problem you've developed. Remember, you are not your addiction! You are something much greater than that. . . ."

But what is it that denial keeps the addict from seeing and confessing? Is addiction a disease or a sin? Does the devil make me do it or am I guilty all by myself?

Addiction: Is it Sin, Disease or a Demon?

To use the word *sin* to point an accusing finger at an addict is as far from the heart of God as one can get. Doing so puts the accuser immediately in the corner of the self-righteous Pharisee whose brand of religion serves to drive the one who feels separated from God even farther away from Him. Members of the Christian community, often frustrated with the repetitive backslider who is really an addict, argue that addiction is sin.

But what about the sincere Christian addict who repeatedly confesses the "sin" of addiction only to fall prey to temptation over and over again? He cannot seem to quit, which would seem to say that addiction is a disease. Yet without exception, every addict I have ever interviewed says that at some point while in the throes of addiction's development he sinned. It is as though he had violated his own moral code which, according to the Scriptures, is sin. "Therefore, to one who knows the right thing to do, and does not do it, to him it is sin" (James 4:17).

This has created what seems to me to be a problem in the addiction-recovery movement, which tends to shun all mention of sin in reference to addiction. In seeking to urge the despairing addict toward recovery, they tend to declare him "not guilty" of wrongdoing and term all addiction a disease. It is hoped that the addict will, as a result of the removal of the feelings of guilt once associated with his "sin" of addiction, find it easier to seek and receive treatment. Yet the most common forms of treatment prescribed by the addiction-recovery movement include the Twelve-Step Program, which involves the admission of wrongdoing. Since sin is a theological and moral issue, let us turn to the Scriptures to understand its meaning.

Sin is from the Greek word *hamartia*, which means "missing the mark." God has circumscribed around every individual a parameter for his life, goals and vision within His will, which will bring him spiritual happiness and eternal benefit. But God has also chosen to give us the ability to choose His will above our own. We can sin not only against God but against ourselves. The job of the Holy Spirit is to tell us when we have "missed the mark" (John 16:8).

Whether a person is an addict or not, he has "missed the mark" God has set for his life because of sin. The Bible says, "All have sinned and fall short of the glory of God" (Romans 3:23). Addiction is but one more way of thwarting God's best for our lives both temporally and eternally and leads to "missing the mark" God has set for us.

Other Christians want to know if addiction is caused by demonic influence. While the reality of demonic influence cannot be ruled out, what about the millions of addicts who have been able to stop without having demons cast out? I believe that the power of demonic influence is manifested in Satan's ability to lure the addict into temptation, the ability to deceive him as to the exact nature of his dilemma and then torment him with repeated accusations of his guilt. These forms of demonic influence are not so easily exorcised as some would believe. Unless the mind, will and emotions are also healed, the addict will continue to repeat addictive behavior or substitute another addiction in its place. The addict may try to turn himself off, but cannot. Demonic forces can then come and go, leaving the addict in despair over his last slip and full of false hope that it will never happen again. The demonic forces take advantage of what the addict unwittingly provides them. But at the judgment seat, it is not demons who take the blame, but the person.

The Destructive Progression

Addiction is but a small part of a progression that leads to an addict's destruction. The apostle James wrote, "But each one is tempted when he is carried away and enticed by his own lust. Then when lust has conceived, it gives birth to sin; and when sin is accomplished, it brings forth death. Do not be deceived, my beloved brethren" (James 1:14–15). We can see the satanic will for destruction in the following progression of nicotine addiction:

1. Appetite

The enemy must find a way to pervert natural appetites and needs. A natural appetite is a God-given desire—for food to fuel the body, sleep, even reading a good book or taking a walk in the woods. A "small pleasure" can become a problem, however, if it begins to be used as a means of escape. How does someone determine if a natural simple pleasure has moved into the realm of unhealthy desire? Perhaps the easiest way is to ask: Does God care? Are there guilt feelings associated with it? Am I trying to hide it from others? If someone's conscience is bothered at all by his actions, it may be that he is moving into sin and needs to take a closer look.

2. *Temptation*

Using natural circumstances such as nervousness, frustration and anxiety, the enemy of our souls makes a play for us by dangling custom-designed, forbidden fruit in the addict's face. Cigarettes become a mood-alterer, producing a calming effect. Some brands of cigarettes are cured with sugar and molasses, tempting the sensitive tastebuds of the sugar addict. Although the beginning cigarette smoker may experience headaches and nausea, these brief discomforts are ignored in favor of the social reinforcement and calming effect brought on by the quickly developing addiction.

3. *Lust*

The nicotine addict learns to crave cigarettes at certain times—after dinner, in social situations where he feels uneasy, when he has time on his hands or when he feels "strung out" with anxiety. At this point, the attraction is no longer curiosity or indulging in the forbidden, but becomes full-blown "lust," translated from the Greek word *epithumia*, which means "a passionate longing or desire."

4. *Sin*

The thought of smoking a cigarette has passed from temptation to lust until the addict reaches the stage of indulgence in the cycle. Regardless of his belief that smoking is wrong, he ignores the voice of conscience and lifts the cigarette to his lips. The nicotine addict who is trying to stop cannot afford one cigarette. The addiction is so powerful that "just one" becomes "just one thousand."

5. *Disease*

Months pass by and instead of cutting down, as the budding addict continually promises himself, he becomes caught in a cycle. He cannot go for more than a few hours or even minutes without lighting up. The smoker's cough greets him, wracking his body each morning. And one year his doctor phones with the news that his chest X ray shows several dark spots in each lung.

6. *Death*

The culmination of the destructive progression is death—in this case, physical death—but in the case of some process addictions, death comes to relationships. Or the addiction takes a destructive toll on one's effectiveness in his or her life's vocation. All addictions are destructive and most have a fatal aspect. One nicotine addict on his deathbed wrote, "I have been operated on for cancer of the lip and larynx. A large section of my face has been removed. But the hole that is left where my mouth used to be is a smokestack. I cannot quit even though by the time you read this I will be dead, a victim of cigarette smoking."

If this sounds preposterous or irrelevant to your situation, be assured that it is not. This progression has already advanced to the disease stage in every type of true addict on the face of the earth right now. For the addict, lust and sin are no longer the central issue. He has long since progressed through these to disease, one step away from death whether it be spiritual, emotional and/or physical. A more appropriate term for the addict's dilemma is full-scale *bondage,* the *enslavement* to a lust. He has lost the power of choice to an appetite, and something is bound to die unless there is intervention.

Addiction, then, involves not only sin but disease. Since Jesus Christ has the answer for both the sinner and the sick, let us not allow semantics to keep us from Him. And God forbid that we in the Church, through our self-righteous frustration, should put a stumblingblock in that path and be the extension of the devil's accusing finger in the addict's face. Let us allow the Holy Spirit to convict of sin and move on instead to healing.

How to Penetrate the Cloud of Denial

The addict lives in a deceptive cloud of denial that must be penetrated with the light of truth if he is to receive help. The process of penetrating this cloud involves five steps.

1. Admit the extent of addiction

For some, it may be easier to confess the "sin" of an addiction than to admit they have become powerless over an addiction. But admitting the extent of powerlessness is a key to breaking bondage. The fact that the Holy Spirit lives in the believer means that the potential to overcome is there, but he has been unable through willpower, self-control, spiritual disciplines and church attendance to control addiction. It has mastered him for the moment. The secret of experiencing *God's* power is recognizing the uselessness of his *own* power.

2. Recognize the urgency of the need to change

Hal, a long-time binge alcoholic, admits readily that he is an alcoholic, but there is no conviction or sense of urgency to change. In the same way that many who pray the sinner's prayer have never been convicted of sin by the Holy Spirit, so the addict may find it easy to admit to addiction. In order to step toward freedom, however, that admission must have beneath it an internal motivation to change.

3. "Own" the addiction

In this step toward breaking the power of denial, the addict must come to the point of accepting the addiction as his own. Rather than blame others, he must accept it in himself. This must happen before he can trust God with it. If it is not really his problem, then it is difficult to hand it to God. Jesus Christ will accept our problems, but first, of course, we must acknowledge that they are ours. We must "own" them before they can be transferred to Him. An addict must accept the addiction as his own before he can give it to God.

4. Take responsibility for the consequences of the addiction

Throughout the course of an addiction, the addict has likely "missed the mark," disappointing himself and harming others physically, emotionally and spiritually. Part of breaking the bondage of denial involves admitting to himself, to others and to God that he has missed the mark. Many addicts testify to the tremendous relief they experienced when they finally accepted responsibility. It was then easier rather than more difficult to move to the next step.

5. Take the responsibility to get help

During the course of addiction, others have urged the addict toward help or abandoned him in their frustration. If denial is to be broken, the addict must now take the responsibility on himself to seek help from counselors, doctors and the Church, as well as to attend support groups in order to follow through with his decision to change.

The Cry and the Sigh

What caused God to decide so suddenly, after the Hebrews had been in Egypt for more than four hundred years, that it was time to deliver them? It was their sigh.

While Goshen had been a resort and the Hebrews had been treated like royalty, living in Egypt was a pleasure—not a tragedy. But under the oppressive authority of a wicked Pharaoh and the lash of the taskmaster's whip, the Hebrews began to break under the weight of their bondage. Why they had come to Egypt was no longer an issue. The reality was that they were now in bondage, enslaved to a power greater than themselves. Only a power greater than the one who bound them could restore to them their freedom. Finally, finally, they began to cry out. And God heard.

In the same way He answered them, He will surely answer one seeking help from an addiction.

In the next chapter, we will continue our journey out of bondage and toward the promised land of normalcy by exploring the second step necessary in breaking the power of addiction: separation.

10
Leaving Egypt—Cold Turkey!

"I never knew how bound I was until I tried to get free!" said Dean, a former well-known gospel music singer and recovering alcoholic. Like many other addicts, Dean was not aware of the magnitude of his problem until he tried to quit. After a relapse lasting over a year, and after a six-month stay in an alcohol-rehabilitation center, and after years of A.A. meetings, Dean began to realize the meaning of the word *bondage*.

He had been the child of an alcoholic and had begun drinking socially in high school. Soon his tolerance increased and he began drinking large amounts in order to produce the same effects. In college he became known as a "boozer." But when he accepted Christ, things began to change. For three years he remained sober, during which time he began a Christian rock band that ministered to churches and youth rallies. But Dean gradually began to wonder if he could handle social drinking since he had been "delivered."

It was not that he denied his alcoholism; he just did not know the true meaning of the word *freedom.*

One night the constant temptation facing Dean proved too much. He took a drink, rationalizing that the Lord had delivered him and that there was no longer any cause for alarm. Very shortly Dean discovered what other recovering addicts know—deliverance from a substance means never using again. Ever! Soon he was drinking heavily. When he was able to stop for short periods, he noticed he couldn't get enough food, particularly sweets. His weight began to increase until his stomach bulged under his stage outfits.

Because of his schedule Dean did not have fellowship with a local church where he would be accountable to close Christian friends and a pastor. When his band cut their own album, Dean felt it was a confirmation that his life was in the will of God because he had made such a success in a short time.

Now Dean was making regular trips to liquor stores and drinking heavily each night in his hotel room. When he began to be late for practices and recording sessions, the manager pressured him. His manager's disapproval was complicated by the frequent blackouts that not only robbed him of his ability to remember where he had been, but also the details of his music. It was then that Dean realized he was back in "Egypt." He had become readdicted to alcohol, cross-addicted to food and sweets, as well as hooked on the "smell of the greasepaint and the roar of the crowd," a curious form of workaholism.

Dean's friends in the music business were afraid to confront him, perhaps for fear of what his absence might do to the financial success of the group. It was a Christian friend of Dean's who was not a part of the gospel music scene who confronted him and urged him into treatment. There, Dean finally learned what it took to really get out of Egypt. Let's see what he learned that brought him to freedom.

Cold Turkey

Modern-day recovering addicts are not the first to discover that separating from the sights, smells, sounds and friends of addiction is a key to recovery. "Cold turkey" was invented by God Himself who chose this method of delivering the children of Israel from the shackles of slavery more than 3,000 years ago. The story of their struggle sends a message to anyone caught in the throes of bondage. It takes power to deliver from power. God chose to separate the children of Israel from the "security" of slavery and place them in a state of dependency upon Him.

Anyone who wants to break addictions will have to make a clean break, too, from everything and everyone that holds him bound. Here is how to do it.

Powerlessness

No one needs a power greater than himself until he finds the humble place of powerlessness. The first of the Twelve Steps of Alcoholics Anonymous says, "We admitted that we were powerless over our addiction, that our lives had become unmanageable." For millions of addicts of various kinds, coming to this simple revelation has required untold human misery. From such addictions as *seemingly* harmless as soap-opera-watching to one as devastating as cocaine addiction, it is only when the sufferer realizes he is under the control of a power greater than himself that he has any hope of freedom.

Unfortunately, much Christian teaching states that in becoming a Christian, a person now possesses a form of omnipotence. He is urged to believe that he can conquer anything alone: "I can do all things through Christ who strengthens me." Here the emphasis is on the word *I*. But only at the foot of the cross do we receive that power. It is not ours alone; it is ours "through Christ." We exchange our weakness for the power of the Holy Spirit. This exchange is necessary to ensure reliance upon God. When we bolster our own egos with Scriptures, we become our own worst enemies.

In order to experience the divine revelation of a person's own powerlessness, God allows that person to encounter situations that "break" him of the deception that he is in control. For Dean, in the story that opened this chapter, that moment came long after salvation, after his relapse into alcoholism. As his condition began to deteriorate, he realized his powerlessness, but when his friend began to tell him he needed treatment for alcoholism, there was still enough left of the Holy Spirit's conviction to reassure him that he was hearing the truth.

As he sat in his hotel room with a bottle of bourbon, he now recalls, "I came face to face with the fact that I was hooked. I couldn't help myself. But at the same moment I knew that God would help me. There was nowhere else to turn. A sense of peace came over me. I cried and cried. It was that experience that gave me the courage to start treatment again."

As the decades passed in the land of Egypt, the Hebrews began to realize a greater and greater discrepancy between the way they were living and their belief that the God of Abraham, Isaac and Jacob was all-powerful. For the Prodigal Son this revelation came in a hogpen far away from his father's house. For the addict it may come gradually or in an instant, but it inevitably leads him to the next step in breaking free.

Turning to a Power Able to Free You

The Hebrews had rallied around Moses when he first returned to Egypt, believing that God had sent him to deliver them from Pharaoh. Lest there be any doubt, however, the Lord allowed Pharaoh's heart to harden. It was the ten plagues that "broke" the Egyptians—*and* the children of Israel. They suffered along with the Egyptians in three of the plagues God sent.

Like the Hebrews, Dean realized that he had to suffer a plague before he could be delivered. "The Lord allowed me to go my own way in order to bring me to the place of total surrender to Him. I thank God I found it out as soon as I did." For Dean the plague of addiction brought him to a greater awareness of the power of Jesus Christ. Dean gave up the idea he could save himself from addiction and changed to *experiencing* the power of Jesus to cleanse him from it. It was this personal revelation to Dean that the same Lord who saved him also had the power *to set him free* that brought him to the next step.

Separation: Rendering Triggers Powerless

The sights, sounds and smells of Egypt tantalized the Hebrews. In the same way, the old familiar places and old familiar faces that accompany memories of addictive experiences have the power to lure the weakened addict into its trap. These are "triggers" to return to addiction.

Studies now underway at the Veterans Administration Hospital in Philadelphia are exploring the phenomenon of triggers in addiction. In a controlled environment, the addict is seated in a room, and furnished with the paraphernalia of his addiction. In the case of cocaine, he is allowed to go through the motions of "freebasing," stopping short of the point of ingestion. In the beginning, the addict's heart pounds; he perspires, overwhelmed by the agony of ungratified craving. But after months of rehearsing the process without gratification, all physical responses subside. The addict is *dead* to his craving. The sensory nerves that once stimulated the pleasure center of the brain are retrained not to respond. This experiment illustrates the power of triggers to stimulate craving.

The biggest mistake addicts make at this stage is assuming that they may attempt to retrain themselves in an uncontrolled environment. The following experiences illustrate the long-standing power of physical craving.

Barbara, a nicotine addict who had stopped smoking for eight years, was chairman of the board of a Christian women's group. After a monthly meeting, a woman approached her for prayer for a nicotine addiction. When the woman handed Barbara her cigarettes, Barbara placed them in her pocket, the same pocket in which she used to carry her own pack and lighter. After the meeting was over, Barbara reached into her pocket, having forgotten about the cigarettes. Immediately the overwhelming urge to smoke returned. Barbara realized, wisely, what was happening and flung the cigarettes into the trash and the craving subsided.

Sandra Simpson LeSourd, a close friend of mine, has been alcohol-free for over nine years. The sight of a TV ad that shows alcohol washing over ice cubes, however, sometimes presents her with a strong craving. In her book *The Compulsive Woman*, Sandy described her return home from a treatment center and the fear of the atmosphere triggering a craving: "Our house was full of old ghosts. Dreadful, painful memories. The chair where I did my heaviest drinking and planned my suicide seemed to menace me each time I passed it. Maybe it should be stored in the basement where I couldn't see it. . . ."

With Charlotte a new Christian recovering from drug addiction who lived with us for four months, the trigger to craving was rock music. Charlotte had cut ties with old friends to move in with us, but in her luggage she brought two crumpled pictures of rock bands. From time to time, Charlotte craved the old lifestyle and the drugs she had given up for Jesus. She would lie on her bed gazing longingly at the pictures, halfwishing she could turn back the hands of time.

Not only is it necessary to recognize the sights, smells and sounds of addiction as triggers to relapse, but also relationships with "Egyptians," people who want to see the addict bound. How awful to think that there are people in a person's life who prefer him to remain as he is, in bondage to addiction, but it is the case. The nature of people addiction or co-dependency makes a person hooked on needy people. When the addict ceases to be a needy person through gradual healing and restoration, a co-dependent often loses interest in the addict. The co-dependent's fear of changing his own crisis-oriented lifestyle causes him subconsciously to promote the addict's dependency in order to maintain the status quo.

One such man drove his wife from an alcohol-treatment center to a restaurant and ordered cocktails. In Dean's case, the members of his band, his manager and other associates in the gospel music world actually preferred to see Dean remain addicted rather than risk hardship that might come if he stopped his hectic, addictive lifestyle and entered treatment. It may take time to discern the difference between healthy and unhealthy people, but such knowledge is crucial to the addict's healing.

Compromise

When Pharaoh began to see God's hand extended against him, he tried to manipulate the Hebrews into compromise. To each compromise, Moses said no. Such must be the case with the addict. His separation from the world of addiction must be total and on God's terms. No wishy-washy obedience.

We are only now unraveling the mystery of the human brain's response to stimulation. In the light of our discoveries, it is little wonder that God chose to sever the Hebrews from all ties with the "triggers" of Egypt. God parted the Red Sea, but only the Hebrews could decide to walk in the way He had opened for them. How does one separate from Egypt? Here are some practical solutions to enforcing abstinence.

Abstinence

Walking out of Egypt means a planned interruption of the addictive cycle through separation from the addictive atmosphere. It means taking a forward look to complete restoration.

During the journey out of addiction God will be there. One way of experiencing His presence is to see the loving incidents that begin to happen: friends who help, the right attendants at the hospital, the answers to small prayers, the easing of pain. In order to abstain from addictive substances and processes, it will be necessary to endure a season of withdrawal. The experience of withdrawal symptoms is a sign of addiction but is the next step after the breaking of denial in beginning a successful recovery.

Warning: Withdrawal from alcohol and other chemical addictions can be not only uncomfortable but fatal unless guided by the care of a physician. Anyone who attempts the following suggestions should first seek the advice of a physician.

Drugs and Alcohol

Cleaning up the addictive atmosphere will prepare the addict to reenter his environment after treatment with as few temptations as possible. All alcohol and mood-altering drugs and chemicals and paraphernalia associated with their use should be disposed of permanently. If he is entering a treatment center, his addiction-cluttered environment will not present an immediate problem, but unless he gets rid of tempting paraphernalia, substances and people, maintaining recovery once he leaves the treatment center will be next to impossible. He should not give away liquor and drugs to old friends who may feel obligated to repay him later on with addictive substances. It is now time to sever all ties with all active alcoholics, drinkers, drug addicts and drug-users. Separating from them by learning to place them on the periphery or completely out of his life rather than as central in his focus, as we will learn how to do in a later chapter, is a vital key to being able to remain sober.

In addition to cleaning up the drug- and alcohol-infected environment, he should enter active treatment. Almost all major hospitals have drug and alcohol detoxification centers as do many rehabilitation centers. If someone believes he is addicted to chemicals such as alcohol and drugs, he should check himself into a "detox" center and place himself under the care of medical professionals. Physical detoxification from alcohol and drugs may last from several hours to several days or longer. Symptoms may include nervousness, irritability, diarrhea, nausea, vomiting, profuse sweating, convulsions, hallucinations and "the shakes." Fortunately, these symptoms are usually short-lived, but some are dangerous and require monitoring by physicians.

This period of detoxification should be followed immediately by a stay in a treatment center. Treatment centers usually have 28-day in-patient programs where individual and group counseling are available, along with movies and activities that educate the recovering addict and his family about the physical, emotional and spiritual effects of addiction. If it is impossible for him to go to a treatment center, he should realize that many major hospitals have drug and alcohol rehabilitation programs, both in-patient and out-patient, as do Veterans Administration facilities. The next best approach is the advice of an addiction counselor, coupled with daily attendance at a support group such as Alcoholics Anonymous or Narcotics Anonymous for a several-month period.

After a treatment-center program, the recovering addict should submit himself to the support of a group such as A.A., as well as active involvement in and accountability to a local church to minister to his spiritual needs. Alcoholics Anonymous does not intend to substitute for a church, but only to help the addict become sober enough to enjoy God's presence and to help him attain and maintain sobriety.

Food Addiction

It is one thing to abstain from a substance that is not necessary to life, but food addiction is unusual in that total abstinence from food is impossible.

In fact, fasting and dieting to control food addiction only contribute to the addictive cycle, the sense of failure and the development of eating disorders such as anorexia nervosa and bulimia. Frequent dieting is actually a form of the binge-purge syndrome, in which the addict eats compulsively for a period of time and then purges himself. Instead of induced vomiting, as in other forms of bulimia, the binge-purge addict starves himself on unhealthy diets. In order to break the addictive cycle of food addiction, it is also imperative to seek the care of a physician to learn how to lose weight gradually and in a healthy way.

Another effective abstinence for the food addict can be through a support group such as Weight Watchers, Overeaters Anonymous or its Christian counterpart, Overeaters Victorious. The principle of the support group is accountability to others about weight and eating habits.

I am 5'4" and weigh 115 pounds at this time, but two years ago I weighed nearly 150 and was moving into a size 16, all this for someone who was so thin she was dubbed "Olive Oil" by her sixth-grade classmates. I know the hopeless feeling of being overweight and too emotionally weak to break the addictive cycle. A trip to my doctor to lose weight started me on a gradual program to lose the extra pounds, but the results of my blood test from that visit frightened me when I discovered my cholesterol count to be 263. Having lost my father and my uncles to heart disease I was urged to take action.

After talking with my doctor and studying several books on cholesterol, I absorbed myself in learning to change my eating habits—forever. Resolutions to "start tomorrow" on various diets had not worked for me, but with the help of my doctor, my husband and family and the information I gleaned about cholesterol, I began to see the Lord's hand in it all. Focusing on lowering my cholesterol as the central issue gradually took the emphasis off my appearance. The diminishing pounds became a byproduct of low-fat, low-cholesterol eating rather than the central issue.

Giving up cheese and throwing egg yolks down the garbage disposal are much easier when your life is at stake! When my cholesterol count finally plummeted to 161 after nine months, my weight was down to 110. Coupling my new eating habits with a regular exercise program three times a week has helped maintain my cholesterol below 200 and my weight at 115. The desire for French fries and burgers has disappeared, replaced by the pleasing taste of foods the way God made them without all that added "sat-fat" and cholesterol. But I still need prayer as do all food addicts who lose weight. Accountability to my doctor, my family and myself not only has helped me abstain but has made a platform for the healing of emotional issues that accompany addiction. In subsequent chapters, we will discuss the healing of the emotional issues, but let us proceed to learning to separate from other addictions.

Other Substances

Someone addicted to nicotine should throw out all cigarettes, lighters and paraphernalia associated with smoking or tobacco use in any form. He should check pockets, briefcases, purses and under furniture cushions for hidden sources of temptation. While nicotine addiction is a strong compulsion, abstinence can be maintained with family and group support and prayer. Compulsive eating is a cross addiction the recovering nicotine addict must guard against.

Anyone addicted to prescription drugs must keep his physician alerted concerning the addiction. He should make an appointment, bring all the medications and follow the doctor's advice. He or she may replace the prescription with a non-addictive one. Physicians are usually not aware that a patient has contacted several physicians to obtain the same prescription. All of them should know so that they may cooperate in the recovery. If a physician does not cooperate in recovery the patient must find one who will.

Caffeine is one drug from which a person may minimize the effects of withdrawal by tapering off gradually—combining caffeinated and decaffeinated coffee in the same pot, gradually decreasing the amount of caffeinated coffee until off caffeine entirely. In *Getting Over Getting High,* Dr. Bernard Green recommends taking a vitamin B-12 supplement, which is non-addictive and non-mood-altering, to replace the false energy once obtained from caffeine.

Process Addictions

In order to break the power of process addictions, the addict has to disassociate himself from everyone who enabled him. This is vital to success. The compulsive gambler will need to toss out all literature, racing forms and odds books as well as disassociate himself from bookies, odds makers and places such as racetracks, lottery ticket booths and casinos. Counseling and support groups are necessary to break the stranglehold of gambling in all its devious forms.

The sex addict must also agree to maintain abstinence in order to have a successful treatment experience. He should avoid pornographic bookstores, "X-" and "R-" and "PG-13-rated" movies and TV programs, peep shows and other places where the temptation to sexual experiences exists. Places where prostitutes hang out must be avoided and phone numbers of ones already known must be discarded. Marital counseling and treatment for unusually frequent sexual activity is crucial.

Sometimes the line between sex addiction and relationship addiction becomes blurred, as it was for Cynthia who was a sex addict before becoming a Christian. But after she first turned her life over to the Lord, she found herself still being drawn to relationships with men to fill the empty places. "If relationship addiction is male and female, sex is always involved," said Cynthia. "I found myself equating the sexual relationship with love, and I was trying to fill my need for love with sex." Getting free for Cynthia meant taking drastic steps. "Abstinence is the only way to stay out of your addiction. I prayed for years about my problems with sex. Nothing really happened until I absolutely stopped seeing and dating men. The only men I could even talk to were my family and my Christian brothers at church. That freed God to start healing me, and He began to fill all the empty places. For the first time in my life, I really felt loved in a complete sense. I no longer need a man to do that—God is sufficient!"

The workaholic must stop compulsive overtime working even to the point of changing jobs, if necessary, to break the addiction. Establishing a schedule and sticking to it is the only way to stop compulsive working. Accountability to family, friends and a counselor reinforces the decision made to budget time. Frequently the workaholic discovers that he has left no time for himself or his family and is heartbroken to realize he has missed some of the best years of his life. Remorse can set him up for vulnerability to other forms of the addictive cycle. It is important that he learn to talk about feelings and to socialize with others, two things the workaholic avoids, in order to break this addiction.

Twenty years ago Vera, now a co-minister with her husband

and a close friend, broke a process addiction to soap operas. "I couldn't do anything or go anywhere for fear of missing my stories. All I could think about was, 'What will happen to Bob and Ellen or Penny and Neal? They ran my life." If Vera happened to be out shopping, she would cluster with other soap opera addicts near the appliance department where TVs were sold to glimpse the characters whose lives she was following. Finally, in Vera's words, "I had to quit watching daytime TV altogether. I couldn't even ask my friends what was going on with the shows or read the updates in the magazines." Now Vera is in a national ministry with her husband, one of the most sought-after ministry teams, because of their humble spirit and powerful work together. But what would have happened if she had not obeyed her conscience?

Your Body, a Temple

When the apostle Paul wrote, "Do you not know that your body is a temple of the Holy Spirit who is in you?" it was one of the strongest images he ever used. Every Jew, as well as every Gentile who had observed the customs of the Jews, knew exactly what he meant. To the Jew, the Temple was a majestic spectacle, honored and revered with awesome wonder. It was the dream of every Jew to celebrate at least one feast in the Temple. As they hiked the paths through the hills and valleys near Jerusalem, their struggle was rewarded with the glimpse of its massive structure gracing the crest of the mountain where Abraham had offered his son Isaac to God. It was holy ground and to this day devout Jews worship at its last remaining wall.

Inside the Temple was a bustle of activity for it was the center of Jewish life. The booths of the moneychangers who exchanged defiled coins for Temple money lined the walls of the outer court filled with pens of the most perfect specimens of sacrificial cattle, sheep, goats and birds. The altar of burnt offering flamed night and day with the sacrifices of repentant Jews scraping together the money to purchase a meaningful sacrifice that would cover their sins. Passing the altar, the men of households could be seen placing their hands on the heads of sheep, oxen and goats and muttering their confessions, their heads bent in worship to the God of Abraham. Worshipers thronged the Temple porticoes. Holy men with their disciples recited Scripture, and the faint smell of incense saturated the garments of the only division of priests permitted in that sacred inner room to minister to God.

Absolutely nothing unclean was allowed inside its gates. To bring defilement into the Temple meant banishment or death, so that an entire division of priests was assigned to keep the Temple undefiled.

So when Paul told the early Christians that their bodies were the temples of the Holy Spirit, it startled them. If the world before Christ had learned holiness from the Jews, how much more should the world after His coming learn holiness from watching Christians, each one a miniature of the awesome wonder of the purity of the Holy Spirit. "You are not your own," Paul continued. "You have been bought with a price: therefore glorify God in your body" (1 Corinthians 6:19–20).

The Christian addict has defiled the temple of his body and for that he pays a heavy spiritual price. He feels the guilt of not portraying to the world the holiness of God. This same sense of guilt causes the *unbelieving* addict to run from the God who could save him. He runs from the joy of God's presence.

What can ensure that joy? The first step is to cleanse the temple, rid it of everything that defiles it.

Through a period of months of treatment, Dean underwent detoxification, but he also submitted himself to spiritual housecleaning, opening his emotions to the healing work of Jesus Christ. While some around him washed out of treatment, Dean walked through the valley emerging with both spirit and body cleansed from addiction. Is he going back to the gospel music circuit?

"For me," said Dean, "my walk with Jesus is more important than making a name for myself." Dean is now a member of a small local church where he is accountable and where he is using his talents to lead believers in worship. Going back to Egypt is the farthest thing from his mind, and he wants to keep it that way.

As Dean learned, separating from the Egypt of temptation is only the beginning of treatment.

Beyond the crossing of the Red Sea lies a wilderness where the addict is placed in a position of dependency on God to move him closer to the promised land. At each camping spot is healing for emotional issues that have always contributed to the addict's dependency on substances and processes. In the upcoming chapters, we will examine these campgrounds of emotional healing.

11
The Wilderness— Pathway to Emotional Healing

Moses and more than two million Children of Israel stood looking back toward the Red Sea. As far as the eye could see, the lifeless forms of men and horses and the twisted pieces of chariots lay strewn upon the beach, the waves gently slapping the remains of the Pharaoh's power.

Pharaoh had lost two key ingredients of his ability to enslave. First, he no longer had *authority* over the Israelites, for they had crossed out of his jurisdiction. Second, and more important, Pharaoh had lost the *power* to recapture the Children of Israel and bring them back; he had lost his army.

As the Hebrews realized the magnitude of the miracle of the Red Sea, they took up the chant of victory and celebrated their newly found freedom. "I will sing to the Lord, for He is highly exalted; the horse and its rider He has hurled into the sea" (Exodus 15:1). In the same way, everyone who steps out of Egypt identifying with Jesus Christ begins to see the power of Satan become a fading memory. Every person who really knows Jesus Christ can testify to changes that took place immediately once the chains of sin were loosened around him.

But even though the former slaves had escaped Pharaoh, they were far from freedom. They were out of Egypt, all right, but there was another phase of God's plan: getting Egypt out of the Hebrews.

The Hebrews found that a wilderness lay between the bondage of Egypt and the freedom of Canaan. Throughout the progress of an addiction, thought patterns and reactionary habits develop that contribute to the enslavement process. When addiction begins, emotional maturing ceases. The addiction becomes the center of the victim's life and causes him to sacrifice everything to obtain gratification. As a result, the addict becomes an emotional cripple, but he is unaware of this; to him being a cripple is normal. Likewise, the addict must make a journey through a wilderness that lies between separation from addiction and normalcy. This wilderness brings the humility needed for recovery.

Recovery is regaining the power to live addiction-free. Rather than referring to themselves as "cured," which gives them an excuse to indulge again, addicts who have been through treatment usually refer to themselves as being "in a state of recovery." A change has taken place but there is more to learn. This acknowledgment is an expression of the essential humility that prevents relapse. Only when the addict begins to feel omnipotent does he begin the landslide toward enslavement again.

Loosening Our Graveclothes

Not long before His passion, Jesus was called unexpectedly to the home of His closest friends, Mary, Martha and Lazarus of Bethany. Lazarus had fallen gravely ill and was near death. Delaying His departure, Jesus and His entourage arrived in Bethany too late—so it seemed—to do Lazarus any earthly good. By the time Jesus arrived, Lazarus had been dead four days. His body lay decaying in its tomb, swathed from crown to toe in a cocoon of graveclothes, strips of linen wound tightly around it and smeared with burial ointment.

But in the hour of deepest despair, the unexpected happened. In a moment of triumph eclipsed only by His own resurrection, Jesus stood outside the tomb and commanded the stone to be removed. Incredulous, the relatives and friends of Lazarus obeyed. Raising His tear-stained cheeks toward heaven, Jesus shouted with a loud voice, "Lazarus, come forth!" And as the crowd of mourners watched, speechless, the man they loved slowly staggered from his "final" resting place and stumbled toward the door of his tomb. When Lazarus was in view, Jesus issued one more command—not to Lazarus, but to his friends: "Loose him and let him go."

For every person rising from the tomb of addiction, Jesus issues the same order to those around him: "Loose him and let him go." Lazarus came forth alive, yet bound with graveclothes. So the newly released Christian emerges from the deadness of his addiction swathed in graveclothes, the things he "got wrapped up in" while he was dead. Addictive habits, lifestyles, hampering traditions, emotional dysfunctions—

147

these are a few of the most common graveclothes. The one newly alive is often so bound that others must help him remove the graveclothes that keep him from walking freely with Christ.

This period of graveclothes-loosening is also the purpose of a wilderness period. In the wilderness, the soul can be retrained to respond to the Holy Spirit rather than external influences. If this sounds easy, think again. The soul doesn't give up that easily but constantly vies against the spirit for control. If the soul wins the battle, it has the power to grieve the Holy Spirit. What is the answer?

The apostle Paul was familiar with the ability of the addictive soul to quench the Spirit: "Do not be conformed to this world, but be transformed by the renewing of your mind" (Romans 12:2). Using Greek words connoting the image of a butterfly emerging from a cocoon, Paul proclaimed freedom through breaking out of the molds in which we have been encased. The Holy Spirit gradually enlightens the understanding and heals the malfunctioning emotions.

The wilderness experience and the unbinding of Lazarus were both unpleasant experiences, but necessary to the release of bondage. The temptation to give up before the intended work had been accomplished was always there. The first temptation of the wilderness experience of Israel was similar to the experience of Derrick, a recovering addict, and his girlfriend, Ruth.

Dealing with Disappointment

When Ruth began attending church, Derrick decided to tag along. Ruth had become interested in spiritual matters through the testimonies of two women in the office where she worked who invited her to a Bible study. At the second meeting Ruth accepted Jesus Christ and was determined to turn her life around. She left the bar scene and immediately stopped having sex with Derrick. But Derrick was one gravecloth that wouldn't unwrap so easily.

Derrick was the child of alcoholic parents. After a stint in Vietnam where he became addicted to both drugs and alcohol, Derrick's emotional scars were deep. When Ruth's life began to change, Derrick determined to hold onto her by turning his life around, too. He quit alcohol and drugs and began attending church services. It wasn't long, however, before Ruth realized that Derrick's "reform" came from the fear of losing her. He had difficulty reading the Bible and almost never talked about the Lord. She felt that the Lord wanted her to end the relationship; finally one night, she was able to muster the courage to tell Derrick how she felt. Derrick stormed out and ran to his old drug dealer, from whom he purchased several "hits" of cocaine. The next week he immersed himself in alcohol and drugs to numb the worst disappointment of his life.

For a while Ruth held onto her faith, but after six months of waiting impatiently for God to move upon Derrick, her countenance began to fall. Why were her prayers not being answered? She was on the verge of leaving the church herself when her friends noticed what was going on and urged her to seek counseling.

Fear of Being Forsaken: The Waters of Marah

Ruth's trial in breaking the relationship with Derrick was emotionally the same one that the children of Israel experienced three days into the wilderness. Exhausted from the desert heat, their water supplies depleted, the Hebrews' joy over their deliverance from Pharaoh began to fade. They were lost. They no longer had a known source of supply. Had they made a terrible mistake? Where was God? Suddenly all the feelings of worthlessness returned. Would it not be better to go back to slavery where Pharaoh had at least provided them with something to drink?

Just when they couldn't go another step, like a mirage before them they saw a spring. The multitude rushed toward the waterhole. But . . . the water was so bitter it was impossible to drink. Disillusioned and angry, the hopeless crowd railed at Moses. Where was God? Did He delight in seeing them suffer? Why did He take the trouble to deliver them and then leave them to die of thirst in the wilderness?

This same terror—the fear of being forsaken—underlies much of man's disobedience to God. More than anything else, man fears abandonment. Ruth and Derrick were both unaware of the fear of abandonment as long as they had each other to lean on, but when the relationship dissolved, the terror became exposed. Derrick returned to his addictions to soothe his aching soul. Ruth, a people addict, was left vulnerable to unhealthy relationships.

A common companion to the fear of abandonment is Satan's whispering accusation that God does not have our best interests at heart. The first person to experience this accusation was Eve in the Garden of Eden. As she drew near the forbidden tree, the voice of the serpent played on her natural hunger. The serpent said, "Has God really said you cannot eat from any tree in the Garden?" When she replied that God had set only one tree apart from them, he pressed again, in order to probe her vulnerability. "You surely shall not die! For God knows that in the day you eat from it your eyes will be opened, and you will be like God, knowing good and evil" (Genesis 3:4–5).

The enemy of our souls lies, claiming that God does not have our interests at heart, but instead sets limits on us to protect Himself. God will abandon me because He does not really care, Satan whispers. And if God cannot be trusted, who can?

In her book *Healing for Adult Children of Alcoholics: How to Break from the Past and Grow Emotionally and Spiritually*, Sara Hines Martin says that the basic emotional issues for children raised in alcoholic homes are abandonment and rejection. "Emotional deprivation is the rule in these homes. The parents are not able to take care of parenting tasks because they are overwhelmed by their own problems. Therefore, nobody raises the children. The children do not get the opportunity to be children." The attention of the alcoholic is on his drinking, not on the children. Because there is a bankruptcy of emotional intimacy, ACOAs fear that they will be abandoned, a condition that promotes the development of addiction.

Mary Tepper, who holds a master's degree in guidance and counseling from the University of North Carolina, Chapel Hill, along with her husband, Elliott, founded Centro Betel, a Christian ministry to drug addicts in Madrid. Mary describes the emotional environment of their quickly growing church, most of whose members are addicts and ACOAs. "You have to teach them the most basic things of caring for themselves. Most of them have very little idea of the meaning of responsibility. To minister to this church is much like living in a house with ninety children."

The children of Israel were like that, too; for them survival itself was the basic issue. They were so damaged, in fact, that only two of the original multitude, Joshua and Caleb, entered the Promised Land. Unlike their peers, they walked through every object lesson in the wilderness with trust and confidence. Patiently they watched as Moses sought an answer to their bitter pool of disappointment.

The press of the people's indignation had driven Moses to his knees. As he prayed, God showed him a way to sweeten the waters so that the Hebrews could drink. The people stood by as Moses cut down a tree and flung it into the bitter water. Suddenly the waters became drinkable, and the Hebrews, forgetting their anger and despair of only a few moments before, crowded around the waterhole to quench their thirst.

But only a few learned the lesson. Those few saw a faithful God willing to change the most hopeless circumstance into their highest good. Most of the thankless crowd, though, saw only a God who must be begged to provide their needs. The latter attitude eventually kept all but Joshua and Caleb from survival in a place where only trust would bring them through.

Ruth

Ruth found counseling and began attending a support group for people addicts, most of whom were children of alcoholics who experienced the same fear of being forsaken. I wish I could tell you that Derrick came back, but he never did. He is still an alcoholic and drug addict, blaming Ruth and the church for his addiction.

But rather than insist that God answer her prayers her own way, Ruth surrendered her "right" to have a man. She went back to college, is now employed as a special education teacher in the public schools and is a faithful member of her local church. Ruth learned to give her disappointments as offerings to God, an act that was central to the healing of her fear of abandonment.

How to Deal with Disappointment

For someone headed for a relapse, *disappointment* is usually the first line of attack by Satan. It is usually accompanied by a desire to return to Egypt.

Disappointment occurs when our expectations are not met. The former slave was positionally out of danger. That is, because he was now in the Lord's jurisdiction and authority, his real "position" was one of a free man. Yet he was still bound emotionally, especially when it came to dealing with the emotion of disappointment. For many addicts like Ruth and Derrick, disappointment is followed by anger, bitterness, fear, feelings of worthlessness and depression, the desire to give up completely. When these negative emotions surface, the addict searching for a "quick fix" is in the habit of turning to his addictive substance or process and becomes sucked into the addictive cycle's destructive tornado. Often before he realizes what has happened, he is sitting on the bar stool, lighting up a cigarette, opening the refrigerator door, walking into a pornographic bookstore or plopping down in front of the TV.

"Disappointments," as someone once said, "are His-appointments." It is important to realize that no circumstance enters our lives without the knowledge of a God who loves us. The apostle Paul was accustomed to experiencing disappointment and wrote, "All things . . . work together for good to those who love God" (Romans 8:28). This theme is also interwoven into the lives of many characters in the Bible. Joseph, the favorite son of his father, Jacob, was sold into slavery in Egypt by his own brothers, where he experienced life-shattering disappointments, which included false accusations of adultery, prison terms and the threat of execution. When he was finally elevated because of his prophetic gift to second-in-command under Pharaoh, he watched as his own brothers staggered into his throne room hungry and destitute. He eventually made his identity known to them and they feared he would take vengeance upon them. Joseph said, "And as for you, you meant evil against me, but God meant it for good in order to bring about this present result, to preserve many people alive" (Genesis 50:20). What Joseph learned is what a recovering addict must also learn: God can take the most regrettable disappointment and paint it into His redemptive plan. The first lesson in dealing with disappointment is to realize this fact about God.

The second step is to guard against that "other voice," which seeks to assassinate God's character in the thought life. Satan, disguising himself in a person's own thoughts, will compare your circumstances unfavorably with that of others, remind you of past disappointments, magnify the worst conditions beyond proportion and assure you that God cannot be trusted. Thoughts like "No one really cares about me," "Nothing ever goes right for me," "Why should I even try?" and "What difference does it make, anyway?" are all thoughts that carry the faint smell of fire and brimstone because they are straight out of the pit. Eroding confidence in God is the intention of Satan in the temptation process. It is at this point that great care must be taken to resist this other voice.

The third step involves offering disappointments to God, surrendering the right to circumstances as he one feels they should be. This amounts to letting Jesus Christ be the real master of one's life. Disappointments are opportunities to give to God a precious sacrifice: having our own way.

The fourth step is to determine to grow up both spiritually and emotionally. Ed Cole, best-selling Christian author and speaker, once said that real Christian maturity was evidenced in the ability to postpone pleasure. The addict's behavior is often like that of a baby who demands that his own desires be met right now. As the child matures, he learns that his own desires must wait. Immature people cannot and do not wait, but mature people can and do.

All of these steps are seldom accomplished without running the gamut of emotions including anger. To ignore the presence of anger or to pretend that it is not there will turn a person into a religious robot. Even the most highly respected figures in the Bible became angry. In chapter 13, we will talk more about anger and the appropriate way to express it. For now, it is enough to admit anger to the Lord over the disappointment and then wait to see what happens!

No one should try to deal with disappointment by himself. It is O.K. to call Christian friends, describe the disappointment and ask them to pray. It also helps to attend a support group and talk out feelings. The recovering addict should avoid people who urge him to use "instant" religious formulas without letting feelings out, or who believe that addiction recovery is an event rather than a process or who encourage him to return to his addiction.

Finally, he should look for—really expect—the intervention of God in the circumstances that follow his disappointment. His way is better than our own. "In everything give thanks; for this is God's will for you in Christ Jesus" (1 Thessalonians 5:18). At the bitter pool of Marah, the Hebrews were not grateful for God's miraculous intervention. They never retracted their angry railings at Moses and at God, but rather swarmed toward the pool, washing their anger down with gulps of cool water. Their inability to humble themselves by admitting that their premature judgment about God was false made them distrust God in other circumstances in the wilderness. The one who learns the lesson at Marah's bitter pool learns to apologize to God and others for his wrong attitudes and resultant misdeeds.

Following these steps will help the recovering addict defuse the temptation to forsake recovery in the face of disappointment and return to an addiction.

But dealing with disappointment without returning to the mood-alterer is only one lesson the recovering addict must learn. There are other major dams on the river of God's healing that must break if the Holy Spirit's power is to flood the landscape and bring restoration. This next lesson is a companion lesson in dealing with disappointment, one of the most difficult to learn but one of the most rewarding.

12
The Role of Fear in Addiction

The first garden my husband and I ever planted was in the backyard of a cottage in Fort Worth, Texas, where we lived while Bill was in seminary. Bill rented a rototiller and spent hours tilling the plot until the tines were buried in the black earth. Nothing green could be seen in that patch and our mouths watered as we planted our seeds, dreaming of all the tomatoes, green beans, onions, peppers, lettuce and okra that would be gracing our table in a few weeks.

It wasn't long, though, before we began to notice green shoots springing up in places where nothing had been planted. It was then that we discovered the plague of every gardener in Fort Worth—nut grass.

"Yep!" drawled the woman at the nursery where we'd purchased our seed, "that stuff's terr'ble! It comes up ever' place. The roots is like nuts that shoot out sideways and make more nuts underground where you can't see 'em. You think you've got it licked and there 'tis again. You can pull it and pull it and them little nuts is still in the ground!"

Bill—a wonderfully patient person—and I—less so—declared war on nut grass. Before we left on our summer mission trip we were winning, but when we returned all we could see of our garden were the tall spindles of okra rising up out of a mass of weeds. It took us forever to bring our garden back into shape that summer. The price was hard work and vigilance.

How many times I have thought about the parallel between nut grass and fears in my Christian life! Fears can so easily spring up just when you think you've got them licked.

The older generation of Hebrews who left Egypt became infested over and over again with their own "nut grass of fear." It lay at the root of every dysfunctional response to God. So, too, is "nut grass" at the center of the addict's scarred emotions. Underneath, where it cannot be seen, fear shoots out its insidious roots, forming new nuts that spring up as anger, perfectionism, rebellion and lack of trust in God.

Fear is the opposite of trust. When fear is rampant, God has trouble leading us. Anyone who cannot trust God will find it difficult to trust other people—and himself. Fear leads to isolation from others, putting them at arm's length, feeling the need to control situations and circumstances and being unable to develop and maintain healthy relationships. Millions of addicts have begun to walk with God, but have been hindered, overcome by nut grass. Let's take a closer look at how fear develops, that we may isolate it and pull it out.

How Fear Develops

Sometimes it is difficult to believe that a "successful" person's life is riddled with fear. Take Sharon, for example.

Sharon, a tall brunette, highly educated in the field of computer technology, is today the chief executive officer of a thriving young company. Married to a lawyer, Sharon dresses for success and lives the lifestyle of a "yuppie." She and her husband rent a restored apartment in the Victorian "charm" district of one of the nation's largest cities. They drive to their offices in matching Mercedes 350 SLs and attend a fashionable downtown church. Sharon accepted Christ through Young Life in high school and has always identified with the Church, even though her parents never did.

Sharon's life was not always the picture of success. She was brought up on the wrong side of the tracks where her father was the town drunk. Sharon never invited friends home, of course. Her home was rundown, her father unpredictable. Often, when he did not like the meal her mother prepared, he would dump the plate on the floor and order Sharon to clean it up.

Sharon was determined to get a good education. Because she was poor, she qualified for grants and used them wisely to enroll in the state university, from which she graduated with honors. In graduate school she met Bob, who was studying law. Their backgrounds and goals were so similar the relationship became serious quickly. They married in a quiet ceremony with a few close friends in attendance. Only later did they tell their parents.

Although Sharon's lifestyle is the envy of many, those who know her do not envy her. Under the guise of overwork, Sharon keeps everyone at arm's length. Her business associates are intimidated by her sharp reproofs. As a result she has no close friends; and recently, communication with Bob broke down as well.

Sharon looks as if she eats sensibly but secretly she binges and purges. She never fits fun into her schedule. She controls every committee of which she is a part—even at church, resorting to the bullying tactics she employs on the job.

Recently, however, Sharon found herself on the verge of nervous collapse. She went to her pastor for help and at first tried to instruct him how best to care for her. In time, though, with her pastor's help, Sharon finally began to discover how she came to be enslaved by her fears.

Fear Produces a Slave Mentality

Although Sharon never saw herself as a slave, she had to deal with the same emotional issues as the Hebrews did in the wilderness. The primary root in her dysfunctional behavior was fear.

As in the life of every fear-entrapped slave, several things had occurred:

1. Her needs were not met.

Slaves are fed and housed only so long as they are valuable to the ruling class. Once they cease to be of value, they are left to fend for themselves. They quickly become self-sufficient, responding to the rule "No work, no provision."

Sharon learned very early to be self-sufficient. Her father was absorbed totally in his drinking and had no way of providing her with the basic needs of praise, security and affection.

2. She was oppressed by authority figures.

As do many ACOAs and addicts, Sharon had a history of being dominated by a ruthless authority figure. Her father betrayed his role as husband and father; and her mother, struggling to keep the family together, had little time for her. As a result Sharon grew up distrusting authority figures. No one except herself was capable of handling authority and she resented being under anyone. As a result, she decided never to be accountable to anyone. Like the Hebrews in Egypt, the only picture of authority she had ever seen was negative.

3. She was abandoned by those she loved.

Sharon was dogged by the fear that she was not worthy of having her needs met because her father and mother were not emotionally available to her and her brothers and sisters were busy fending for themselves. In marriage Sharon even learned to live in isolation from her husband.

4. The home in which she grew up was governed by the four key fears.

Sharon's home was governed by *the fear of facing the truth*. Her father was the town drunk but to face this truth was out of the question. Marrying in secret was only one instance of her inability to face her family's homelife.

Her home was also fraught with *the fear of fellowship*. Sharon's mother avoided social contacts and gatherings, isolating herself in her home. The children were never allowed to invite anyone over. They were allowed occasionally to attend birthday parties, but only if they came right home. As a result, Sharon was isolated physically and emotionally. It taught her to avoid situations in which she might be vulnerable to hurt or where people might find out what her past was like.

Sharon's family was also ruled by *the fear of communication*. Her family was silent, not in the habit of talking about their problems, as every family member was expected to resolve his difficulties alone. They never mentioned her father's alcoholism, which seemed too big to handle.

And finally, the family's *fear of change* was so deep-seated in Sharon that for a long time in counseling she denied its existence. She always envisioned herself as a "mover and a shaker" committed to change to keep her company competitive. But as the mystery of her past was unraveled, Sharon began to see that the fear of change lay at the root of her desire to control everything and everyone around her.

The presence of each of these fears produced in Sharon the inability to trust anyone. She had to control her environment. Although she was an excellent manager and planner, qualities a highly successful executive must possess, she went beyond this to applying the laws to personal relationships as well. It was the only way she felt comfortable, which led to her desire to cling to the work atmosphere where she felt safe, the only environment in which she knew how to cope.

Sharon was angry with God because with Him she was out of control. She could not trust God and wait for Him to work any situation out. She felt she needed to step in, "putting feet to her prayers," as she usually said.

Breaking the Grip of Fear

Through counseling, Sharon gradually opened herself up. The following is what she learned that led her to relax her grip and let God show her what He could do when she released control.

Learning to trust God

In order to break the former slaves of the belief that their destinies were in their own hands, God had to lead them through a landscape where there was no visible supply, not even food or water. The wilderness that separated Egypt from Canaan was a wasteland. With a long journey to make, their life was nomadic, moving from campsite to campsite, staying in one place as long as the cloud of God's presence hovered over them. As soon as the cloud moved, they moved. It was the only canopy that sheltered them from the harsh desert sun. The shifting cloud seemed to be without control or direction and the multitude of ex-slaves became uneasy once again. *What are we going to eat? Will there be enough water?* And as the miracle at Marah faded in their memory, the Hebrews began to wonder if they would have provisions again.

I used to believe that the wilderness was forced on the Hebrews to purge them of wrong attitudes, but I have since begun to wonder if the wilderness doesn't more accurately represent all "current circumstances." There will always be vicissitudes in life. We even joke about them. I know one man who whenever he cooked chili wore an apron inscribed with the phrase *Into each life some rain must fall—but this is ridiculous!* I wonder now if the troubles of life are not the normal terrain, an environment we must pass through. There is no way to avoid trouble. Deaths occur in everyone's life, financial losses, sicknesses, misunderstandings between friends—all of these sprinkle the lives of everyone, Christian and non-Christian.

But properly handled, these everyday wilderness experiences give us a chance to walk through tough times holding the hand of God.

That's what trusting Him is like.

Much has been written in Christian circles about faith. It has been touted as a commodity, something we can purchase from God with the stress and strain of grunting it up. Some even suggest that the denial of rough terrain makes the journey easier and eliminates the obstacles in our pathway.

I don't think so. The Bible describes faith as both a gift and a fruit, something that eventually occurs as a byproduct of the Holy Spirit's presence. While we have the ability to let the nut grass choke it out, faith is there because it was given to us by God. What makes the difference then? Why is one Christian defeated while another one is victorious?

The Difference Between Faith and Trust

The answer lies in understanding that while faith is something God does, trust is something *we* do.

Faith is a noun only, but trust is both a noun and a verb, an action word. Trust is something you decide to do. Trust is placing your confidence in God and leaving it there regardless of the rough terrain. But how do we do that?

1. Decide to trust. Instead of letting the status of the terrain determine how we will feel, the trusting person *decides*, on the basis of God's nature, that he will place his trust in Him.

2. Let go and trust! In order to trust, we must haul off and do it! This usually happens the moment we make our decision.

3. Keep our trust anchored in God, no matter what. Instead of giving in to spiritual exhaustion, to worry, anxiety, dread and fear, we must not move our trust out of God. When the anchor is secure, we will eventually ride out the storms, regardless of momentary stumbling and feelings that we won't make it.

4. Face fear. Putting our trust to work has its greatest challenge in facing fears. Irrational fears stand in the way of God's will. Most will disappear as we walk through them with confidence in God, but those that do not should be handled with counseling.

It doesn't matter how weak a person is, it is where his trust rests that determines whether or not he will eventually make it through rough times. For the addict climbing the terrain of emotional recovery, the way may be slow, but will inevitably lead to the top.

The hungry Hebrews with pangs gnawing at their stomachs began to look not forward but backward. They remembered some of life as it had been in Egypt. "If only we were back in Egypt, where we sat by the flesh pots and ate bread to the full." Forgetting the nightmare of slavery, their stomachs screamed for instant gratification. Soon not only their stomachs but their voices were screaming in unison.

Again Moses sought God and told the Hebrews to get ready to see His provision. As the dew fell, God Himself deposited a food, rich in nutrients, tasting like wafers with honey and of such miraculous nature that everyone from the child to the largest man ate the same amount and did not get hungry. Their own puny abilities to help themselves were not sufficient. It was God who brought them out and God who would bring them through.

Learning to Trust Others

Learning to trust God is only half the battle. Learning to trust others is another victory for the recovering addict. The secrecy of addiction usually includes shutting others out of one's private life. As Sharon, in the story just recounted, entered counseling, she recoiled when her pastor asked her to begin attending a support group. This was agony for a woman who had grown up believing she did not need anyone.

It took six weeks of meetings before Sharon could start talking about her feelings. To her, a person who talked about feelings was weak; she had to humble herself and confess her attitude to the group before she found much freedom of expression, but it finally came. Now Sharon can't believe she ever made it as long as she did without others. She has made several new friends as she let her guard down, trusting God to help her through the rocky terrain of developing relationships.

But one of Sharon's greatest benefits from counseling has been her newfound ability to accept her limitations. A once hopeless perfectionist, a malady we will discuss in chapter 14, Sharon used to hate herself, set such high goals that they were unattainable and feel guilty when she fell short. She has begun to trust God with *herself*. At this writing, Sharon is not nearly as obsessive about her weight as she once was and has begun to make her relationship with Bob a higher priority than her career. She no longer works overtime and is free to go out for frozen yogurt and a walk on the beach. "I know I have a way to go—but I'm never going back to the way I was. I'm beginning to love the life God gave me." For Sharon, breaking the powers of fear and self-sufficiency made the difference between a happy life and an unhappy one, between the bondage of process addiction and the ability to live addiction-free.

The next step in emotional healing for the addict may be the most crucial. All addicts must deal with the next hurdle in order to recover. It is the underlying factor in compulsivity of every kind and a primary key to self-control. Let's see what it is and how to deal with it—God's way.

13
Rage in Addiction: Healing Hidden Anger

It was September 19, 1985, and the day was just breaking through the haze over Mexico City. Taxis and cars were jammed six and seven abreast at busy intersections. The rush hour was just beginning and the work force of the largest city in the world was flowing into the arteries leading into the downtown business district.

No one noticed that the birds weren't singing.

Ann McKay, a veteran retired missionary visiting friends in their apartment several blocks from downtown, told me how she sat in her bathrobe ready to drink her morning coffee. Suddenly, the brown liquid began to slosh in the cup. For a few moments Ann was puzzled until the sound of cracking began. Having lived in Mexico before, Ann scurried for the nearest doorway to brace herself for the usual tremor. But this time, according to an article in the May 1986 National Geographic, seismic waves one thousand times more powerful than the atomic bomb pulsed through the dry lake bed underneath Mexico City. The ground rippled at a speed of 15,500 miles per hour. Registering 8.1 on the Richter scale, the tremor was so strong that it shook the plate glass windows in downtown Houston and sloshed the water in puddles in Colorado. Four minutes later when Mexico City had come to a halt, 9,000 were dead. Ann emerged unscathed, thanking God to be alive, the building where she stayed only mildly damaged.

An earthquake is one of nature's most frightening disasters. While it knows no equal in natural disasters, it has a striking parallel in human emotions. An earthquake's soundwaves emanate from its focus below the earth at a decibel range undetected by man until the surface quake begins. Anger, too, begins long before the outburst occurs. Anger gains momentum as it builds until it erupts in a hot, pulse-quickening release of violent energy. An explosive outburst of anger has the capacity to destroy both the one who releases it and the one victimized by it. But long before the outburst occurs, symptoms show its presence in a hidden, festering form.

It is festering anger—what I call "swallowed" anger—that presents the greatest danger to the addict. I have found from my own counseling experience that anger, in its hidden form, is the very springboard of compulsivity. Beneath a calm countenance is a closet full of unacknowledged, unreleased anger.

Swallowed Anger Always Present in Addiction

Although not everyone who has hidden anger is an addict, I have never seen an addict who did not suffer from unreleased rage. The person who swallows his anger is much like a man who eats tainted food in a restaurant and hours later vomits it up in another place. The victim of an angry person is usually not the cause of his anger. The anger was swallowed when it should have been released safely and appropriately. In the beginning the tainted food is not detected. It may taste normal, but eventually the effect will be waves of nausea until it is expelled.

Here is a checklist for symptoms of unreleased anger. Check the symptoms you know you have.

Symptoms of Hidden Anger

_____ 1. Are you frequently depressed?

_____ 2. Do you have any of the following stress-related physical symptoms: sore back and neck muscles, facial tics, spasmodic foot movements, habitual fist clenching, stomach ulcers, pains in the back, neck and abdomen, anxiety-produced numbness, blackout spells or chest pains, frequent tiredness due to anxiety-produced muscle tension?

_____ 3. Do you have sore jaws or clenched jaws? Do you grind your teeth—especially while asleep?

_____ 4. Do you frequently experience physical symptoms undetectable by your doctor?

_____ 5. Has your doctor ever told you that you have a psychosomatic illness and are experiencing actual symptoms induced by your emotional state?

_____ 6. Are you sleeping for unusually long periods to escape unpleasant situations or thoughts?

_____ 7. Do you become habitually drowsy at inappropriate times?

_____ 8. Do you become unusually irritated over trivial matters?

_____ 9. Are you moving in slow motion?

_____10. Do you put off completing necessary tasks?

_____11. Are you habitually tardy?

_____12. Do you joke compulsively to the point of boring your audience?

_____13. Do you habitually cut yourself down verbally?

_____14. Is your humor sadistic, stabbing at others with jokes containing hidden barbs?

_____15. Do you have bizarre thoughts you are afraid of but may never even consider carrying out, such as murdering your family members or committing suicide?

_____16. Are you sarcastic, cynical or flippant in conversation?

_____17. Do you sigh frequently?

_____18. Are your emotions numb?

_____19. Do you have nightmares and strange dreams in which you are personally endangered or in which violence occurs?

_____20. Have you become bored or apathetic lately, experiencing loss of interest in things you once enjoyed?

_____21. Do you have difficulty getting to sleep at night because of angry or tension-producing thoughts?

_____22. Do you awaken in the night with your mind actively mulling over events and worries?

_____23. Do you smile when you are hurting emotionally?

_____24. Do you laugh when nothing is funny?

_____25. Do you usually effect a mask of cheerfulness and politeness when you feel sad or angry?

Score: Use this test as a guide to help you understand your emotions and the potential for hidden anger. Answering yes to up to five questions could indicate anger ready to tremor; six to ten yes answers suggest the emotional equivalent of a San Francisco 7.1 on the Richter scale—moderate damage; eleven to fifteen yes answers could mean you are headed for an 8.1 Mexico City quake and may blow up causing a lot of damage; and sixteen or more yes answers place you in a serious condition, much like a national disaster looking for a place to strike.

Anger Is a God-Given Emotion

Anger is the emotion you feel when your will is crossed or your rights have been violated or you have been victimized.

Anger in itself is not evil. It is, in fact, a trait of God Himself that He has given to man. When it is employed for the purpose of releasing frustration, and experienced properly, it can be a learning experience.

The first mention of anger is in the book of Genesis. It was Cain, the son of Adam and Eve, born after the Fall, who is first mentioned as experiencing this emotion. Cain and Abel had both brought sacrifices to the Lord. Cain's sacrifice was an array of vegetables picked from his fields. Abel chose to sacrifice from the firstlings of his flocks. The Scripture says, "And the Lord had regard for Abel and for his offering; but for

171

Cain and for his offering He had no regard" (Genesis 4:4–5).

Was God playing favorites? Why did He refuse Cain's offering? The types of offerings the two men brought revealed much about the brothers. Abel recognized the depth of sin and offered the best he had—"the firstlings . . . and the fat thereof." It was a sacrifice of atonement—shed blood—and since we learn from Matthew 23:35 that Abel was a righteous man, we can discern that his heart was in the right place in coming before God.

Cain, on the other hand, brought of the fruit of the ground—as commentator Matthew Henry explains, anything that was readily available that he did not need. He did not approach God in faith with regrets for the magnitude of his sin.

When Cain realized that God had not regarded him and his offering, he felt scorned, insulted, rejected—and angry. But instead of using his anger as a signal that God had something to teach him, he held it in. God even sought to encourage him to learn from this experience, but Cain would not listen. Days passed as he seethed in his anger and bitterness, maintaining his "cool" yet with a discontented countenance. When he finally could stand it no longer, he rose up against his brother and killed him in a fit of rage.

Do anger and sin always go together?

It was Paul who said, "Be angry, and yet do not sin" (Ephesians 4:26). Notice that he did not say, "Do not be angry because it is sin," and yet that is the erroneous interpretation we live. Other Scriptures exhorting the believer to put away anger, to disqualify leaders who are given to anger and to keep one's temper under control are frequently read to mean that no anger is appropriate. As a result, many Christians live their lives trying to swallow anger in the hope of eradicating it from their emotional repertoire.

Some have been taught that God is the only one qualified to get angry because His is the only righteous anger. But we feel anger nonetheless. Anger is a God-given emotion that when vented properly releases tension. Only when it is stored and released improperly does it become perverted and destructive.

The Addict's Closet Anger

Radio fans remembering the series "Fibber McGee and Molly" often recall with amusement the sound of Fibber opening the living room closet. As the door squeaked ajar, a torrent of rattling, clanging and banging sounded as junk fell out. In the same way, the addict has a closet of junk stored away from years of anger-producing events. Anger left overnight undissipated ferments into bitterness. When Paul wrote, "Do not let the sun go down on your anger" (Ephesians 4:26), he was referring to the tendency of anger to turn to bitterness.

Swallowing anger, deciding to think about it later, delaying the feeling and expression of this emotion stores up layers of hostility. Sometimes the anger is released around "safe" persons or those whom you know cannot challenge you. They become the victims of your fermented hostility. But often closet anger seeps out into the human personality and behavior in various ways wearing different masks.

The Many Faces of Hidden Anger

The following is a partial list of several of the masks commonly used for closet anger. Perhaps you have known people like this or recognize these symptoms in yourself. Toward the end of the chapter we will discuss the appropriate expression of anger and how to get rid of what is already there.

The *King Saul,* who vacillates between periods of normalcy and rage, often becoming provoked to violence or near-violence by trivial matters.

The *Jezebel,* whose deep rage manifests in the ability to manipulate circumstances and people to one's own advantage.

The *Victim,* often a people addict who allows himself to be abused and harbors an often numbed and therefore hidden form of rage.

The *Angry Prophet,* who stores up his anger and releases it against causes, religious and social evils and others who do not hold his views.

The *Judas,* an enraged zealot who, when disappointed by an authority figure or co-worker, will feign loyalty while going silently for revenge.

The *Pharisee,* who takes subconscious pleasure from self-abasement.

The *Moses,* a person in leadership who is pressured unjustly by the complaints of the spiritually immature and who, as a result, accumulates a backlog of rage in his emotional closet. The inappropriate release of that swallowed anger can cause him to miss his "promised land."

The *Talking Serpent,* who, through gossip, subverts the confidence others place in the individuals with whom he is angry.

The *Despondent Clam,* who is unable to express his views and feels frustrated at being manipulated.

The *Compulsive,* who often punishes himself by indulging in things his conscience does not permit as an act of anger or spite against God and other authority figures who disappoint him.

The *Impulsive Risk-Taker*, who, to prove he is not worth anything, traps himself in a prison of circumstances from which he cannot quickly extricate himself.

The *Sweet Smiler*, who never allows any display of anger to emerge and is often unaware of feelings of anger, having shoved them down for so long he cannot feel them.

The *Mummy*, who has decided not to show anger, and because of this decision has also shut down every other emotion—love, joy, happiness, peace.

The *Complainer*, who has a pessimistic outlook as a result of his anger toward the hurts and deprivations he has suffered in life.

What's wrong with these masks, which the addict is so expert at wearing, is that they are forms of blatant dishonesty.

Not every angry feeling can be vented immediately, of course. And it is true that tact can avert a blow-up. But that doesn't mean *hiding* how we feel; it only means being appropriate. We should let people know our reactions, but not always by being angry. Dr. Theodore Isaac Rubin, a well-known psychiatrist and author of *The Angry Book*, writes, "Negate anger and you must also negate love. Love requires a real self and a real exchange between real selves. People who are not themselves, who are acting a part, cannot make a real exchange. They can only act." To deny the expression of anger is to deny ourselves as God made us, to pretend that we are something we are not. Christians, in trying to mimic what they believe to be biblical principles, are often acting out a false spiritual role where not only they but the people around them cannot be real.

An addict, full of emotional turmoil, can play this game just so long before he lapses back into his addiction. It was phoniness in others that made Jesus angry—not an honest admission of need.

Helping the Addict Take the Power Out of Anger

Although anger is a Godlike emotion, when it is stored up it becomes a gravecloth that must be removed. "Let all bitterness and wrath and anger and clamor and slander be put away from you, along with all malice" (Ephesians 4:31). The words *put away* here come from the Greek root that means "to be lifted away." To be lifted away, anger must be recognized, gradually accepted and released. Here are the steps in detail:

1. *The addict must learn to recognize his/her anger.*

Long before the earthquake does its damage, its sound is heard by birds and animals sensitive to its decibel range. Recognizing anger by knowing its symptoms and faces should alert the addict to the fact that anger is stored in his spiritual closet. Denial keeps anger in hiding. Recognizing it is the first step to being free.

Not only must he recognize stored anger, but he must also learn to recognize the anger that may enter his life *today*. As soon as he senses the disturbance of peace in his spirit, he should look for anger and for its cause. By the time he feels anger or recognizes its symptoms, it is too late to cut it off; it is there in his soul. There is no point in pretending he is not angry. God has already heard it in his spirit as a bird or an animal feels the low murmurings of an impending earthquake.

2. The addict can then accept his/her anger.

After anger is recognized, he must accept the fact that he has it. When God saw that Cain was angry because his sacrifice had been rejected, God Himself approached Cain and said, "Why are you angry? And why has your countenance fallen? If you do well, will not your countenance be lifted up? And if you do not do well, sin is crouching at the door; and its desire is for you, but you must master it" (Genesis 4:6–7).

The addict can use anger to learn something about his own heart. It is only when the human heart is tested by circumstances that we find out what is in it. He should try to answer God's question "Why are you angry?" Is it because of closet anger or immediate anger? Why did the addict become angry? What portion of his will was crossed?

If he doesn't know, he should answer God's second question, "Why has your countenance fallen?" Why is he wearing a mask? Denial must be broken before he can experience cleansing. He may need to write out the things he still holds in his closet. These would be anger-producing events over which he never allowed himself to express his feelings. He can write out what was done to him and ask himself why he is still angry about it. Is it because a wrong was committed? Is it because his pride was hurt?

In making the list, it is likely that he will begin to experience the feelings of anger. As he does he is ready for the next step.

3. The addict can then release it.

The Scripture says, "Be angry, yet do not sin." The way a person releases anger determines whether or not he enters into sin. Inappropriate release occurs when he victimizes a person, calls people names, insults them, uses foul language, takes God's name in vain, threatens or frightens people, manipulates them or harms them physically. The hot-tempered man who habitually flies into a rage has not learned to express his anger appropriately.

But what then is the appropriate way to release anger?

It is to allow ourselves to feel the anger. Feel the quickened heartbeat. Be aware of tears or trembling or raising our voices a few decibels. It helps to describe those feelings. If someone condemns them we can remind him or her that we are simply following the pattern of Scripture to "be angry, yet . . . not sin." While feeling anger is not a sin, storing anger overnight and allowing it to become bitterness is. "Confess your faults one to another, and pray one for another, that ye may be healed" (James 5:16, KJV). We must accept the fact that we have been angry. We can get angry today and will probably be angry tomorrow; that is human.

One good way to express our feelings is to God in prayer. King David, who was called "a man after God's own heart," learned the art of touching God with his emotions. There was no emotion he was unable to express in the presence of God. The Psalms are full not only of his love and joy, but also his anger and desire for vengeance and vindication. Look at Psalm 140:9–11: "As for the head of those who surround me, may the mischief of their lips cover them. May burning coals fall upon them; may they be cast into the fire, into deep pits from which they cannot rise. May a slanderer not be established in the earth; may evil hunt the violent man speedily." Since vengeance is God's responsibility, such prayers are entirely appropriate. It is the person who thinks he must hide his negative side from God who winds up feeling separated from

Him. It is all right to cry out, to let out an outburst while God listens in. After all, He heard it deep in our spirits.

The addict should begin to describe the anger-producing event to God, the reasons why he is angry and what he wishes God would do about it, how he feels frustrated because he can't do anything about it, and how he wishes that he could "punch their lights out!" In the beginning he may feel uncomfortable doing this, but if we can't tell God how we really feel, whom can we tell?

The first time I tried this I was afraid. But I decided to "let her rip" anyway. In the middle of my outrage, something wonderful happened. I began to experience the sense of God's pleasure in a startling way, as though I had broken through a mask of denial that had separated us as friends. In the presence of the Lord is fullness of joy, wrote the psalmist (Psalm 16:11), and I was amazed to experience joy suddenly in the midst of my anger.

In many of David's psalms in which he expresses his anger, the last verse is one of peace. "I know that the Lord will maintain the cause of the afflicted, and justice for the poor. Surely the righteous will give thanks to Thy name; the upright will dwell in Thy presence" (Psalm 140:12–13). David experienced this peace by releasing his anger in the presence of a mighty God who could handle it. It is one of the highest expressions of faith to acknowledge that God knows all about me—even my anger, bitterness and hatred—and He loves me just the same. This revelation is what the writer of Hebrews meant when he wrote, "For we do not have a high priest who cannot sympathize with our weaknesses ["the feeling of our infirmities," KJV] but one who has been tempted in all things as we are, yet without sin" (4:15).

But what about expressing anger directly to a person you are angry with?

Jesus did. He became so angry with the Pharisees on more than one occasion that He scowled at them, raised His voice at them and called them names. John the Baptist got angry, too, and so did the apostle Paul, whose heated argument with Barnabas resulted in periodic separation. To the one who is a true friend, an occasional expression of anger—even a heated one—can clear the air and be used as an opening to greater understanding.

It is also appropriate to express anger when a loved one is endangered physically or spiritually by his actions. If a child disobeys a parent's instructions about running out in the street, placing metal objects in electrical outlets, treating his parents and others with disrespect or maliciously destroying the possessions of others, he deserves not only to see his parents angry, but to be disciplined appropriately and, yes, even spanked as a manifestation of love. Remember, if you don't punish him now, the police will later. If a parent is not carrying around a closet full of hidden anger, he will not cross the line of discipline into child abuse.

Learning to adjust anger to the situation is also a necessary art. Does the infraction warrant a release of anger in the offender's presence? If so, what form should it take? How intense should it be? Giving some thought before releasing anger is entirely appropriate. Regardless of how we express anger, it is wise to be cautious. The apostle James wrote, "Let every one be quick to hear, slow to speak and slow to anger; for the anger of man does not achieve the righteousness of God" (James 1:19–20). Thus, the addict who maintains his anger finds himself falling short of the righteousness of God. As the addict learns to deal appropriately with anger, he will find himself becoming slower to anger. "He who is slow to anger is better than the mighty, and he who rules his spirit, than he who captures a city" (Proverbs 16:32). The one who is slow to anger has his closet empty of swallowed anger. Once his closet is empty, it is much easier to be patient and understanding with others, using a soft answer to turn away an unnecessary outburst of anger.

The purpose of anger is to vent a human emotion that cannot be held in without causing trouble; it is never to work the purposes of God. Decisions should never be made in anger, for words spoken in haste can leave scars that may never be erased. It is unwise to express anger toward those in positions of authority such as a boss, the civil authorities or leaders in the church. Any angry words spoken other than to vent your emotion—such as insults or character judgments—need to be retracted and apologized for in order to restore relationships. In the midst of anger, the righteous man must learn to "bridle his tongue" (James 1:26). As the bridle is used to channel the horse's energy and ability in a constructive manner, so the one who channels anger constructively, learning to stop short of verbal abuse, can occasionally use anger to a constructive end.

It is not wrong for the recovering addict to feel anger, and the one whose emotions are being healed will find that his feelings of rage are less frequent and shorter in duration. As his closet is emptied of hidden anger, he becomes free to use his emotions rather than be controlled by them. If he uses anger properly, it can lead to real, lasting forgiveness.

4. The addict can then deal with forgiveness.

The proper form of anger can lead to better relationships for the addict if its release includes this final step of forgiveness.

In fact, forgiveness is difficult only when he harbors closet anger. Trying to forgive when anger has not been acknowledged is nearly impossible. In ignoring anger, he ignores a lesson God wants to teach. Once anger has been properly released in God's presence, he is free to forgive, letting go of ill will and misunderstanding that have been too quickly stashed into the closet.

Once he has released anger, he should be able to approach the person(s) who have angered him and discuss the problem without excessively volatile emotions getting in the way. In this way, God's righteous purposes can be worked. It is much easier to change when the addict is not defending his pride. Without first emptying anger, though, such attempts result only in fake politeness. Once he has been able to forgive—not only with a conscious decision of the mind, but with the emotions—he should not keep thinking about the anger and let it find its way back into the closet. Rather he should focus his attention on matters at hand and the joyful living of life today. "Be kind to one another, tender-hearted, forgiving each other, just as God in Christ also has forgiven you" (Ephesians 4:32). A good follow-up is a genuine, emotion-felt deed of kindness, keeping a sensitive heart and a forgiving spirit.

Learning to use anger rather than abuse it is a key to addiction recovery. The next step in our journey through the wilderness brings us to a particularly devastating form of self-deception, common to all addicts.

14
The Addict's Particular Battle: Overcoming Perfectionism

Consider the answers to this quiz:

Perfectionism

_____ 1. Do you often *feel* joy at the gut level?

_____ 2. Do you often compare yourself negatively with others?

_____ 3. Do you frequently postpone the completion of projects because there's just not enough time to do them the way they should be done?

_____ 4. Do you usually feel genuine joy when you hear

that someone you know has accomplished a goal you've set for yourself?

_____ 5. Are your goals usually too unrealistic to be attainable?

_____ 6. Do you have difficulty receiving compliments from others?

_____ 7. Do you often feel frustrated because you are just not accomplishing enough?

_____ 8. Do you enjoy your accomplishments?

_____ 9. Does your pace of life bring you to a period of "burnout" cyclically?

_____10. Do you *feel*, overall, that God is pleased with your performance so far?

_____11. Do you feel like a motorboat being driven at full speed or like a sailboat driven by the wind?

_____12. Are you afraid to try because you are afraid to fail?

_____13. Do you withhold approval from others who do not meet your expectations?

_____14. Do you tend to set aside relationships with people who do not meet your expectations?

_____15. Do you feel that "it's hard to get good help these days"?

_____16. Do you feel that you need to "justify your existence" by accomplishing goals?

_____17. True or false: Nothing should be done in an average manner.

_____18. Do you feel that issues are usually black or white, one way or the other, without any gray in between?

_____19. Are the words *do it right* frequently in your observations and conversations?

_____20. Do you have trouble apologizing to others for
your mistakes?

_____21. Are you afraid of making decisions for fear of
making the wrong one?

Score: The perfectionist will answer no to questions 1, 4, 8
and 10, *motorboat* to question 11 and yes to all the others. If
you gave perfectionistic answers to at least five questions, you
might be considered mildly affected. If you responded with
six to ten perfectionistic answers, you are likely developing a
problem that needs attention. If you answered from eleven to
fifteen questions with perfectionistic answers, it is possible
that your relationships are drastically hindered by perfectionism. More than sixteen answers very likely indicates that you
could benefit from professional or pastoral counseling and
maybe a support group.

Perfectionism: The Addict's Religion

The addict is particularly subject to a devastating heresy. It
is one that has been around for thousands of years: "We get
our salvation the old-fashioned way—we earn it!" This was
the motto of the Pharisees of Jesus' day. Jesus came to deliver
mankind from this very brand of religion. Centuries of having
the Law of Moses interpreted by uninspired men had reduced
Abraham's knowledge of God to little more than a painstaking
observance of thousands of regulations, the slightest infraction of which could mean spiritual defilement. It is tough to
live under the concept that God is a giant Rule-Maker, pushing you onto a tightrope from which you're bound to topple.
Not only were the Pharisees proponents of this form of faith,
but so, sad to say, are many Christians today.

Perfectionism lies at the root of this form of religion. Perfectionism believes that man is not worthy of God's love; he must *prove* his worth. That teaching is not real Christianity. The message of Jesus Christ is one of unconditional love that saves us and then presents us faultless before the Father. His Gospel is not based on our own doing, but on our acceptance of the blood of Jesus Christ shed for our sins. Once a person is a Christian—tacky or pretty, flawed or flawless, addicted or not—God has taken responsibility for him. Christianity is not something you do; it is who you are.

And perfectionism—the heresy—is, more often than not, the addict's religion.

Perfectionism is taught by people who put conditions on their love: "If you don't do it right, don't do it at all!" or the subtle, unspoken message, "If you're good, I'll love you." The addict tends to carry this attitude over into other areas including his relationship with God. What results is a sense that he must prove he is worth something.

Note that true perfectionism is not simply the performance of a job to the best of one's ability, a godly trait. Perfectionism is the debilitating malady that keeps us from feeling acceptance.

Symptoms of the Addict's Perfectionism

Some symptoms of this malady are low self-esteem, a sense of rejection, feelings of insecurity, the fear of abandonment, jealousy, closet anger, pride, the inability to accept the flaws of others, the inability to admit error in oneself and a crippled inability to feel God's acceptance.

Many addicts were reared in homes in which they were taught they could never measure up to their parents' expectations. Anger over not being perfect and thus not being able to gain approval has wrapped itself around the addict's soul. As long as frustration over imperfection remains, the addict's perfectionism becomes a trigger for relapse. It causes him to break relationships with other "imperfect" people. It gives little margin for error in others while glaring errors remain in himself. It causes him to be irritable, impatient and compulsive and leads to the development of workaholism, one of the most common process addictions.

Sometimes perfectionism was not taught to the developing child by parents but through "significant others" such as teachers, pastors, Scout leaders or peer groups who withheld their acceptance and approval. But where did this strange religion come from in the first place?

Back to the Fall

Before the Fall, God created man and placed him in a vast Garden. God gave man the physical, emotional and mental prowess to care for such a place without producing even the tiniest drop of sweat upon his brow. The pre-Fall state of man was what we could call *super*-natural. When Adam and Eve sinned, they lost the ability to enjoy the Garden in such a way. Adam now had to battle the weeds and thorns, and earn a living by the occupation that once came so easily. Much of Adam's effort was now focused on protecting his family from the results of the curse they had brought upon themselves. In his quieter moments, Adam surely longed for his pre-Fall abilities and the sense of God's presence and protection that now seemed so far away.

I believe that perfectionism is the latent desire of the Adam in all of us, especially those of us who are addicts, to return, *through our own effort and ability*, to the super-natural capacity man once had when he looked after the perfect Garden of Eden. Perfectionism is man's attempt to recover from the Fall. He tries to do this by himself, without the blood of Jesus. He is unwilling to accept the limitations, flaws and imperfections that are now a part of life. Perfectionism is a form of rebellion that keeps addicts from accepting their weakness and their utter dependency upon God. Perfectionism is their counterfeit for the "rest" of God. The perfectionist wants to achieve through his own efforts, in a sense to be like God—to be perfect.

Low Self-Esteem: The Root

Healthy self-esteem is the ability to see ourselves as God sees us. The Hebrews camped outside the border of the Promised Land of Canaan eager to hear the reports of their new homeland from the twelve spies that Moses had sent across the border. Soon tiny forms appeared on the landscape and the congregation ran to meet them. But their eagerness was short-lived.

As each of the spies gave his account, he told of the beauty of the land, displayed the giant-sized cluster of grapes and bore witness to the fact that Canaan was, indeed, everything God had promised—with one exception. Populating this wonderful place were tribes of giants so large that the tiny Hebrews shrank into insignificance in their presence. "We became like grasshoppers in our own sight, and so we were in their sight," sighed the spies (Numbers 13:33). But more than the size of the giants, it was the general small view of themselves and their lack of confidence that God could help them complete the task that ground the entire camp to a halt.

Only two of the spies, Caleb and Joshua, encouraged the people to trust God and take the land.

Likewise, it is our own low self-esteem that causes us to shrink back in fear from the promised land God has planned for us. This is the attitude of the frustrated perfectionist. His nagging sense of inadequacy and his fear of failure both shrink him in the face of any challenge. The idea that we must be perfect before we can try is the attitude of the perfectionist. Until we are perfect, we will fail. We must not, therefore, attempt anything—even what God tells us to do—until we are bigger, better, more qualified, more educated, better-looking, more spiritual, (fill in the blank), perfect. But the fear prevails that we will never be better than we are, so we are trapped outside the promised land.

The truth is that we do not inherit the promises of God on the basis of *our* merits, but on the basis of *grace*. Grace is not earned. Grace is a gift, which can only be received.

The reason the Hebrews failed to go in was that their vision was wrapped in the gravecloth of low self-esteem, the inability to see ourselves as God does. Their low perception of themselves constituted a form of pride because it stood in the way of God's will. They were afraid to try because they were afraid to fail.

Perfectionism is a malady that occurs in the addict in active form—continually striving; and passive form—giving up because he knows he will never be good enough. It is the principal factor in a particularly devious form of addiction we have not yet mentioned: religious addiction.

Religious Addiction

The religion addict is a well-meaning, usually sincere individual whose soul and spirit are both so tightly wrapped in the gravecloth of perfectionism that the joy of knowing Jesus escapes him. He may not be a born-again Christian at all, but a counterfeit, substituting powerless godliness for the true knowledge of Jesus Christ. If he is a Christian, the religion addict manufactures a heresy of co-salvation. He preaches grace but lives life on the principle of salvation by works. The story of Bruce is a vivid but all-too-common illustration of the heartbreaking danger of religious addiction.

Bruce was a college student when he first came to Jesus Christ. After a death in the family, Bruce came face to face with the reality of life and death, quit boozing and began attending a fellowship not far from the university he was attending. Bruce seemed to grow spiritually, devoting himself to helping the small church get started. But as time passed, Bruce found it more and more difficult to stay away from his old ways and eventually he went back to the life of alcohol, marijuana, sex and drugs.

Six years went by as the church gradually grew to a congregation of a hundred members. Sometimes the pastor would remember Bruce, wonder what had happened and pray for him. One day, much to the amazement of everyone in the church, Bruce returned. Another brush with death had frightened him into reality, and he returned to the church and took up where he left off.

This time Bruce wasted no time in making up to God, to the pastor and his Christian friends for his six years of backsliding. He attended every service, worked at the church, drove the elderly and the sick to doctors' appointments and made himself available to the needs of everyone.

If Bruce had been faithful before, his life could be characterized now only by the word *devout*. He absorbed himself in the Bible, committing Scriptures to memory and soaking up the Old Testament with meticulous care. Soon he was like a walking concordance, able to sprinkle his conversations liberally with references to the Word of God.

But the Bible was not his only devotion. Bruce took seriously the scriptural injunctions to pray and fast. Those closest to him began to notice that he fasted often, sometimes for weeks at a time, and prayed many hours a day. All of these disciplines made the members of Bruce's church believe that he was no less than a modern-day prophet, committed to the Lord and to the church with unusual piety.

Then the trouble started. Those who admired Bruce put great stock in his leadership. They organized a prayer group whose purpose was to seek God until revival came. The pastor, seeing nothing wrong, gave it his blessing and the group began to meet at the church building. Some did not understand praying prostrate on the floor and the frequent calls to fast, but others who sincerely wanted to do all that was necessary for revival cooperated eagerly.

One night when the pastor came to the meeting, he was hit with the realization that all was not well. His presence was not welcome. His attempts to pray were drowned out by those lying prostrate on the floor. When the meeting was dismissed, he called Bruce to his office and began to talk to him about the direction he and the group were taking.

Bruce's countenance was doleful and pale, and his hands trembled as though from weakness. There was an intense, morose, stern air about him. Refusing to answer any of the pastor's questions, Bruce began to give the pastor what he believed was a harsh word from God: "Repent, or God will remove His glory from this church and judge you for your faithlessness!"

In the coming weeks, despite all efforts to talk to Bruce,

the chasm widened. Soon Bruce spent the Sunday school hour in the prayer room; and during the worship service, as the charismatic congregation paused for the ministry of the gifts, Bruce began to give out his harsh "prophecies." In a few weeks, the division in the church was complete. In a fury of righteous fervor, Bruce and his group challenged the leaders to dismiss them from the fellowship. Shaking the dust off their feet, Bruce and his disciples, all of whom were addicts and children of alcoholics, many of them emotionally vulnerable women, left the church and started their own group.

The story ends sadly. Five years later, Bruce and his slowly diminishing group have roamed from church to church, endearing themselves to unsuspecting pastors and then "prophesying" against them. The greatest tragedy has not been the damage done to the churches, but the deception that has overtaken Bruce. Instead of the joy of knowing the real Jesus Christ, Bruce has substituted a false fervor. He is filled with rage that God has not answered his pleas for revival. Blaming this unanswered prayer on the imperfect leaders around him, he continues his role as "the angry prophet," launching a one-man clean-up campaign for the Body of Christ. In his attempt to recover from his addictive lifestyle of the past, Bruce has substituted a cross-addiction to religion, the religion of perfectionism.

But Bruce's example is not the only form of religious addiction. False religious experiences and counterfeit fervor are only two of a chain of symptoms that indicate the presence of a cross-addiction many turn to when recovering from the other substance and process addictions. Always the root is perfectionism, the nagging fear that they have not done enough for God, that He is demanding a standard of holiness so exacting that without strict observance they will miss out on God's best for their lives. It is this phenomenon that Stephen Arterburn refers to in *Growing Up Addicted*. "Frequently people will 'get religious' and believe they are growing spiritually. They merely improve their respectability by wrapping the church and religion around themselves. What may result, rather than spiritual growth, is a form of compensation that produces religiosity or religious fanaticism."

The following is a list of symptoms of religious addiction.

Twelve Symptoms of Religious Addiction

1. Self-Atonement

The religious addict is preoccupied with atoning for his past wrongs. Since he cannot accept himself as an imperfect individual, he must atone for his mistakes over and over again. The religious addict tries to wash away sins already cleansed by the blood of Christ. Whether it is attending church obsessively, going to confession compulsively, as Martin Luther did before his conversion, or resorting to extreme spiritual disciplines, the religious addict does not feel forgiven, so he turns to works.

2. Isolation

The religious addict becomes set on a course of spiritual pride that eventually leads him to isolate himself from a healthy group of believers. He begins to feel that his devotion is greater than that of others in the fellowship, and that he must separate himself "unto God" by isolating himself from others.

It is this tendency that causes the vulnerable person to

unite with a cult group which, although it may have many members, is isolated from the rest of the Body of Christ.

3. Superior revelation

Unlike someone led by the Spirit of Christ, who is humble and teachable, the religious addict becomes controlled by false revelation and false doctrine, twisting Scriptures to throw like darts at the flaws of others. He may be given to manufacturing false wonders and ghoulish manifestations and hearing voices. These manifestations do not usually bring glory to Jesus and often have the ring of truth but without mercy.

4. Rejecting authority

When rebellion wears a religious cloak, it usually rejects authority. The perfectionist is dissatisfied with less than perfect leaders. Any flaw is magnified. Because experiencing the grace of God is foreign to the perfectionist, he cannot trust God to move through others who do not deserve mercy. I have often observed that a person raised in a dysfunctional home is looking for the ideal parents he never had in the pastor and his wife. When they disappoint him by not living up to his expectations, the perfectionist frequently discards them, disqualifying them to be his leaders.

5. Martyrdom and suffering

The religious perfectionist usually has a persecution mentality. This manifests itself in a desire to punish himself or atone for the sins and misdeeds of others. The religious addict will ultimately believe he is a martyr, called to suffer for his high calling. All attempts at correction from others in the

Body of Christ are viewed as persecution or the inability to understand his difficult calling in life.

6. *Judgmental spirit*

Picking the lint off the Body of Christ is the chief preoccupation of the religious perfectionist. Seldom does he take joy in what is right. The religious perfectionist devotes himself to cleaning up the Church. He believes that the responsibility rests on him, sometimes him alone, to do what others do not have the courage to do. Hidden anger always seeks a victim, and in this case his victim is what he believes is the "lukewarm" Church.

7. *Pious mask*

Religious addicts, like the Pharisees of Jesus' day, "broaden their phylacteries, and lengthen the tassels of their garments" (Matthew 23:5). This spirit loves to display itself. Some sects of Christianity forbid women to wear makeup, earrings and colorful clothes, desiring that their separation be visible. Other religions compel their followers to don a certain garb to separate them from the crowd. The countenance of the religious addict is usually devoid of joy, often glassy-eyed. His intense, dramatic stare and stern look complete the sanctimonious garb of the Pharisee.

8. *Losing touch with reality*

As the religious addict absorbs himself in prayer and the Scriptures, his false revelations lead him to lose touch with reality. He is lost in the "spiritual realm," seeing those things "into which angels long to look" (1 Peter 1:12). He has little time for worldly distractions and starves his soul of pleasure. He finds it difficult to talk about normal or natural things. He spiritualizes Scriptures so that the literal meaning is obscure. He may experience auditory hallucinations masquerading as the voice of God. In its extreme manifestation, these hallucinations can lead the religious addict to fast himself to death or kill others in the name of Christ.

9. Numb emotions

The anger of the religious perfectionist causes his emotions to become numb. Realizing he is vulnerable to hurt as a result of being "called" to this difficult task, he no longer allows himself to feel anger, but he does not feel joy or love, either. He becomes led by duty and obligation alone. This inability to feel enables the religious addict to become quite ruthless. Jesus promised the disciples that their enemies would "kill them thinking they were offering service to God" (see John 16:2). Religious addiction makes this possible.

10. Extreme practice of spiritual disciplines

Prolonged fasting, prayer, worship and frequent, extreme sacrificial giving (such as giving away the money for rent and bills, life savings, inheritances "in obedience to the Lord") are symptoms of religious addiction. Usually these demonstrations are seen by others and become ways of "sounding the trumpet" as Jesus said the hypocrites do. Instead of these disciplines leading the perfectionist to Christ, Jesus becomes more obscure as other religious or church-related issues replace Him. These extremes lead the victim to lust after the effects of spirituality rather than walk in humility, the love of Jesus Christ and the love of the brethren.

11. *Control and manipulation of others*

The religious addict is sometimes a person who has the capacity to influence others. The religious addict may lead the vestry, be the voice of the board of deacons or be a spiritually minded person who gains the respect of the congregation. He will inevitably exert that influence in the wrong direction, pulling away from the pastor and other leaders.

12. *False fruit*

One of the most obvious signs of religious addiction is the absence of the real fruit of the Holy Spirit. In spite of the presence of gifts, zeal and dynamic ministry, which may seem to be present, the religious addict is bankrupt of love, joy, peace, patience, kindness, goodness, meekness, gentleness, self-control. In their place are often artificial fruits that include the ability to sway people emotionally, a syrupy sweetness, numb emotions, obligatory sacrifice, a compulsive sense of being driven toward spirituality, a false meekness that turns attention to himself, and an air of pride and superiority. This motivates the religious addict to be legalistic, domineering, insistent on his own way and emotionally immature.

The victims of religious addiction are under a special form of stress. Having experienced emotional trauma in which they felt alone and afraid, they turn to religious form to calm themselves. The Christian *should* turn to God's fellowship, but the religious addict turns to religious practices. The religious addict follows the addictive cycle, using religion as his process addiction. Of all the process addictions I have encountered in our church and in my counseling, this is the most tragic because it keeps the addict from the true source of joy, an alive relationship with the risen Lord.

Religious addiction is one of the most prevalent forms of perfectionism. Practically every church has encountered this phenomenon in various degrees and fumbles for a label for it. It is as common as the other addictions mentioned in this book.

The Effects of Religious Perfectionism

According to Dr. David Seamands, Christian author and psychologist writing in *Healing for Damaged Emotions*, this is what a religious addict usually faces: "Under the stress and strain of trying to live with a self he can't like, a God he can't love and other people he can't get along with, the strain can become too much. And one of two things can happen: either there is a breakaway or a breakdown."

The breakaway perfectionist is one who has given up trying to be perfect. The woman who can't keep house perfectly and resigns herself to living in a mess is an example. So is the ACOA who can't feel God's approval and leaves the Church to go back into the world.

The breakdown perfectionist may face a long, slow spiritual burnout in which disillusionment and hidden anger overtake the frustrated Christian—sometimes the minister. Or breakdown may occur with the emotionally fragile perfectionist who cannot handle the intense fear of abandonment and the frustration of trying to be perfect, talk perfectly and act perfectly.

In either case, God does not answer the perfectionist's religious exercises because to do so would simply promote what is false. God holds back until the perfectionist is tired of trying to look after Eden in his fallen state. When he runs or breaks, he may be ready for the solution to his problem.

My Own Encounter with Religious Addiction

The reason I know about religious perfectionism is that I have experienced it firsthand. I have faced religious addiction and seen its devastating effects.

A number of years ago, I became enamored of the idea of revival and began to devote myself to seeking it through prayer and fasting. I fasted for three-day periods, seven-day periods, twenty-one day periods and forty-day periods. All I got was hungry.

During these times I became intense, absorbing myself in the Old Testament without balancing the view of God through studying the New Testament and the life of Christ. I, too, like Bruce, felt that God was speaking messages of judgment to others, which I delivered with zeal and white-knuckle obedience. All this time, a souring was taking place in my heart. The joy left and I began to feel numb. Unrecognized, as yet, was a closet full of anger and rejection that I was taking out on the Church.

No, I didn't become a perfectionist because of my parents. It probably began as a reaction against never having been popular at school. Perfectionism dogged my footsteps and escalated as I moved slowly into this deception known as religious addiction. In 1980 I began to experience pains in my stomach and sought medical attention. Nothing was organically wrong and yet the pain was intense. One day while I was crying out to God for healing, God began to touch my perfectionism.

The past ten years have brought me through several difficult lessons that have begun to counter the poison of perfectionism. I have begun to experience the grace of God myself as I have sought to edify the Church rather than criticize and judge it.

The message of grace has been a particularly liberating one for me, for it was this revelation of Jesus Christ that eluded me during my years as a confirmed perfectionist. At times I have felt as though I were pushing out the power of perfectionism by overindulging in the grace of God, a fear that is real to many perfectionists. *I'm concentrating too much on grace, and not enough on obedience,* I would tell myself. But it has been grace alone, ministered to my aching spirit through members of the Body of Christ, that has relieved the emotional pain.

Since my fasting became a cover for an eating disorder (I would binge and purge through fasting rather than vomiting), as an alcoholic cannot take a drink, I cannot fast. Even one meal into the fast and the sense of heaviness and perfectionism overtakes me, sucking me into the addictive cycle. But God has taught me the joy of simple, quiet obedience rather than earning His approval through fasting.

One night as I lay in bed thinking about grace, I began to understand that God's perspective included the reality of my shortcomings, and that He saw me through "grace" glasses. As a spectator walks into a 3-D movie and is handed a pair of glasses with which to appreciate the third dimension, the dimension of depth, so the Lord hands every Christian a pair of grace glasses when he walks into the Church. Without these glasses, it is possible only to see with natural eyes in limited two-dimensional viewing. But with grace glasses, we are able to see others and to see ourselves with God's perspective because He wears them, too.

If we want to *be seen* through grace glasses, we must also *wear* ours. When we remove ours, we have the sense that God has removed His and all the old feelings of perfectionism return.

Grace glasses are not meant to reinforce denial. Instead, through them we can see everything even better than with the naked eye, but with the added dimension of grace. When I wear them, my eyes are able to rest from all the stark perceptions of the natural realm—judgment, criticism, perfectionism—and enjoy the added dimension of seeing others with the grace of God.

When I wear the grace glasses, I see the new parameters that God has set for me. I do not have to accomplish my goals perfectly. When I wear the glasses God gave me, I can see my efforts hindered by my fallen mind, will, emotions and body. But that's all right. God sees these faltering efforts, too, through the wonder of grace glasses.

I have decided that I never want to take them off!

For the addict who recognizes tendencies in himself toward perfectionism, here are some steps to freedom.

Prescription for Addiction to Perfectionism

1. Break denial.

Anyone who is tired of performing for God, for others and for himself must first experience the breaking of denial and be set free.

2. Confess pride and unwillingness to see and admit error.

This is extremely difficult for the perfectionist. He often confesses sins such as throwing his gum wrapper on the sidewalk and ignores sins like unkindness or rejecting authority. Perfectionism is the enemy of real confession of sin because it renders its victims fearful of admitting error. To admit error is to have failed, the thing the perfectionist fears most.

3. Right wrongs.

Perfectionism blocks repentance and restitution, but self-abasement is no substitute. Once the place of real repentance is found, restitution is the next step. Going to those the perfectionist has judged and accused wrongly will shatter any remaining denial and cause the full light of truth to shine in his heart. He should find out from them what he can do to restore the broken relationship and then do it. This thwarts the devil's attack in isolating the perfectionist from the Body of Christ.

4. Submit to your church and its leaders.

The perfectionist-addict has been so afraid of commitment as to reject the very thing that is at the heart of Jesus Christ: unity. As he gives up his perfectionistic expectations of the church and its leaders, trusting God to handle them, he will realize the need to be taught the truth by those who have known Jesus much longer than he has. An attitude of submission does not seek to control and manage, but to fit in.

5. Walk in the light you have been given.

This is extremely important for the perfectionist. He is not responsible for walking in the place the Lord has shown someone else. He should not place restrictions and demands on himself because others do unless he is convinced it is scriptural and what the Lord wants him to do.

6. *Drink in heavy doses of the grace of God.*

The addict needs to eliminate judgment and criticism from his heart and mouth. Because he has been so crippled by this deception, he must realize that God will not use him at this time to minister correction to the Church. The grace of God is an unearned favor. It is not for sale, and he cannot buy it. It may take years to begin to be healed of the scars of perfectionism on his spirit. But when healing is complete, his compulsions will subside, his emotions will be restored to full, healthy function and he will so much enjoy ministering grace that he will shudder to think about the way he used to perceive God and others.

While his emotions are still in a fragile state of recovery, he should sit under those teachers who preach and live grace, whose attitudes are balanced and not condemnatory. I had to stop reading certain authors, even well-respected and well-known authors, whose books were loaded with perfectionistic admonitions and restrictions. It was also necessary for me to drop my name from the mailing list of a particular evangelist whose self-proclaimed prophetic denunciations sounded spiritual and holy but lacked the proper mixture of grace and truth to be edifying.

7. *Relax and be led by the Lord.*

It is not easy for a religious addict, a workaholic or any other kind of perfectionist to relax, but it is necessary for healing. We can take a lesson from elephant seals, some rather homely creatures who have something to teach the one who is worried that God isn't pleased with him. The elephant seal is a sea creature who spends six months of the year swimming in the ocean and the other six lying on the beach shedding his skin.

These are the only things this creature must do in order to please God. Swimming and sunbathing are the things he does best, the things he was created to do.

The one tending toward perfectionism should consider what he was created to do and to be. He can take a hint from hobbies and talents. Maybe he doesn't paint well enough to win a blue ribbon, but the fact that he has even a small talent invested in him is a cue that God placed it there for enjoyment.

He should start having fun. The addict or the child of an addict usually has a dysfunctional "fun-haver." Because he takes life and himself so seriously, he does not have time for clean pleasure. The soul starved for it has denied a part of himself that God created. It is fine to go to church prayer meetings, but he should go to the parties and picnics, too. He can take a vacation. If he fails to give himself respite from work and soul-searching, he will miss life. My mother says, "Don't get so busy you don't have time to live."

She's right; she's 81 and she knows.

As the graveclothes of denial, fear, self-sufficiency, anger and perfectionism are gradually peeled away, the recovering addict is able to rise up and, like the Prodigal Son, return to God. In the next chapter, we will discuss what it takes to restore that relationship.

15
Restoring Fellowship with God

Once again the story of the children of Israel is the addict's story.

As the Hebrews walked through the wilderness separating them from the Promised Land, it became apparent that they were still addicted to Egypt. For 430 years (more than twice as long as the United States has been a nation), the children of Israel had felt separated from God. First, in the days of Joseph and shortly thereafter, there was the lure of living in a resort-like land where every need was gratified immediately . . . a period not unlike the beginnings of an addiction when all seems rosy. Then came the nightmare of slavery that crushed their spirits and caused them to believe that God had rejected them. Their cries went unanswered for centuries—until one day God acted.

In the space of a few weeks, they emerged from Egypt. Moses led them through the same wilderness where he had led his father-in-law's sheep. There God began to show them that only through submission to Him was there any hope of inheriting the Promised Land. At each camp, the multitude thinned as the wilderness claimed everyone who would not learn. At the foot of Mount Sinai, the Hebrews encountered one of their greatest tests. It was there they learned just how much God wanted their first allegiance.

Moses ascended the mountain, with Joshua following some distance away. He was on his way to meet with God having accomplished what God had told him to do—bring the Hebrews to the mountain to meet the God whose power had brought them out of bondage. Tragically, the people had decided they didn't want to meet God, only to speak to Him through Moses. So as Moses ascended the mountain leaving Aaron in charge, the multitude went about its business instructed only to wait until Moses' return.

Forty days elapsed and still no Moses. Fear that he had died stirred the fear of abandonment in this multitude of former slaves. The stress began to eat at them until the band of pilgrims erupted into an angry mob. They confronted Aaron, demanding to go back to Egypt, the only place they had ever felt secure. Fearing the throng, Aaron cooperated in their plan.

As a godly few watched in horror, this mob that the God of Abraham had chosen for Himself prostituted itself in one of the worst demonstrations of idolatry and revelry in all the Word of God. Having watched the Egyptians, they knew what to do. It was in Egypt that they learned about idolatry and about drunkenness on a national scale. Under Aaron's direction, the women tore off their earrings and jewelry and piled them in a heap. He took the gold, melted it down and formed a golden calf, an image of a god in Egypt, to be the center of their festival.

The people went into their tents, broke out the stores of food and alcohol they had brought out of Egypt and began to indulge in every form of lust they knew: gluttony, illicit sex, drunkenness and idol worship. This single day of national sin so weighed on the conscience of Israel that the apostle Paul commented on this incident in his letter to the Corinthians: "Now these things happened as examples for us, that we should not crave evil things, as they also craved. And do not be idolaters, as some of them were; as it is written, 'The people sat down to eat and drink, and stood up to play' " (1 Corinthians 10:6–7). This nation was in full relapse to all the addictions of Egypt.

As the people reveled in their iniquity, Moses stood high on Mount Sinai holding the two stone tablets on which God, in His own handwriting, had written His Law. As the people's sin became apparent, Moses broke the two stone tablets. In a fit of righteous anger he came down, burned the golden calf, ground it to powder, scattered it over the water and made the sons of Israel drink it. Then he gave them a choice: "Everyone who wants to follow the Lord, gather to me." As priests separated from the crowd to Moses, he ordered them to kill everyone not standing for God, and so it was that three thousand died who preferred their lustful lifestyle.

Addiction and Idolatry

When I asked Dr. Ronald L. Rogers, a psychiatrist certified in addiction medicine, what he would include in a Christian book about addiction, he answered, "I would include the disease concept of addiction, the importance of grace in recovery, the Twelve-Step program and the concept of addiction as idolatry." M. Scott Peck, well-known psychiatrist and author, would agree that addiction is idolatry. In an interview for the March-April 1988 *Changes* magazine, a publication for Adult Children of Alcoholics, Peck made the comment, "All addictions are forms of idolatry."

An idolater turns to his idol to replace a deficiency in himself, whether it is peer pressure, nervousness or a lustful natural appetite. Idols are our own making. They represent what we think God looks like, what we think He should be like and what He should do for us. The problem is that an idol is not the real God.

Idolatry is a religion learned from parents and others in the idolatrous culture. From observation we see what it means to follow idols and how they are used as substitutes for God. We learn to turn to them in times of stress instead of to a loving God. *Addiction is idolatry, turning to something or someone other than God to fill a need.*

The Separating Power of Guilt

Idolatry is a sin. It is a clear violation of the commandment "You shall have no other gods before Me" (Exodus 20:3).

And sin brings with it a sense of guilt and shame, which has the power to separate us from God. An addict, caught in the ever-repeating cycle, proceeds from stress to indulgence, remorse and denial. Instead of dealing with guilt appropriately through God, the addict returns to his substance or process. In the case of chemical addiction, he is driven by physical craving that spins him in the direction of his idol. His willpower proves ineffective. A pervasive sense of guilt manifests itself in the addict's inclination to be secretive about the rituals of his addiction.

What makes a person feel guilty? It's his conscience. Every

man's conscience senses right and wrong. Before Jesus Christ comes into a life, the conscience operates according to what society taught him and what he decided to believe. After Jesus Christ comes in, the conscience is activated when he has done something that grieves the Holy Spirit.

The Scriptures exhort us, "Grieve not the Holy Spirit of God" (Ephesians 4:30, KJV), which means to make Him sad. It is also possible to sin against one's own conscience. It is in this way that the addict feels guilty. His conscience tells him that he is doing wrong, and he feels a pang of sadness whenever his conscience is violated. Repeated violations produce a calloused conscience that does not operate properly. It gives up, not bothering to signal the person anymore. Instead, the sense of guilt manifests itself in avoidance of God and others whom he knows he has wronged.

In order to be restored to God, we must deal with real guilt. It has the power to keep us separated from God and from others until we face it, look for its roots, bring it to Jesus Christ and leave it behind. Even false guilt must be recognized. The principal symptom of false guilt is avoidance of God. It keeps us separated as much as the real thing. The guilty person does not pray, sing, get much out of Bible reading or have any desire to attend church, as illustrated by the story of Barry.

Barry, a recovering alcoholic and a Christian, entered a treatment center for alcoholism one dreary December day. He had become withdrawn, sullen and depressed, hiding from those closest to him the fact of his addiction. Even though he was only in his twenties, Barry spent a year in treatment. For a person who was not disposed to sharing, treatment was difficult.

In Barry's words, "I had to work through a lot of guilt,

shame and anger. How could I do this?" His sense of guilt at having violated his own conscience heaped a heavy load of guilt on his soul.

"What helped me was becoming more aware of what alcoholism is. I'm an alcoholic, not a bad person. I had to learn to accept it, work on it and to manage it. Then I could like myself."

During treatment, Barry stopped going to church. Just *beginning* to open his closet of hidden anger took nine months because he was so fearful. When Barry finally did open up, it was a matter of weeks before the doctors were talking of dismissing him. Then Barry asked his parents to bring his Sunday suit because he wanted to go back to church. "I had to work through some anger before I could pray," said Barry, explaining his months of silence toward God.

Barry illustrates the addict's separation from a *relationship* with God. He did not want to talk to God. When a person is trying to avoid God, the last thing he wants to do is to pray. "Beloved, if our heart does not condemn us, we have confidence before God; and whatever we ask we receive from Him, because we keep His commandments and do the things that are pleasing in His sight" (1 John 3:21–22). The converse is also true. Whenever we are not keeping His commandments and not doing the things that are pleasing in His sight, our heart condemns us and we have no confidence before God. But once healing begins, addicts can approach God with a sense of confidence and acceptance.

In order to find this sense of confidence and acceptance, the addict must deal with perfectionism, the attitude that says I must do something before God will accept me. The secret of a good relationship with God is the one King David had—talking with God regardless of what he had done or how he felt. When the addict can similarly express anger in God's presence he is well on his way to healing. When he is hiding, he is carrying a load of guilt and a defiled conscience and won't be able to pray until it's removed.

Dealing with Guilt

Guilt feelings are God's warning signal that it is time to bring a wrongdoing to Him and lay it on the cross of Jesus Christ. God knows that no one can approach Him and enjoy His presence while in a state of guilt, so He has made provision for this: We can accept the blood of Jesus Christ as atonement for our wrongdoings. Once the exchange is made, there *is* no sin. And there is no guilt since, according to God, they are one and the same. Not guilty! There is no longer any need to feel guilty because guilt, in God's eyes, is no longer there.

To have this exchange work properly, it is necessary to recognize exactly where the sin lies. Although chemical addiction is a physical problem, disease-like in nature, it was the "turning to" a substance or process instead of to God that made the addict feel guilty in the first place. This is no surprise to God. He already knows about it. But the addict needs to tell God he feels guilty, that he wants to be healed, forgiven, so that he will no longer violate his conscience. He must admit his powerlessness and turn—not to the addiction, but to God to restore him.

Remorse is not enough. Remorse is pride-centered. "How could I have done that!" Repentance is change-centered: "I don't ever want to do that again." Remorse is what the Bible calls "the sorrow of the world," which produces death. Remorse is a stage of the addictive cycle. If an addict wallows in remorse, he will either fall into depression or begin to feel that he can lick the addiction on his own. But if remorse leads to repentance instead of denial, he will interrupt the addictive cycle and start on his way toward freedom.

Repentance comes from the Greek word that means "to turn around and go back," to make a 180-degree turn and begin to go back the way we came. It means to stop what we are doing, return to God and accept His prescription for freedom. Repentance does not involve self-sufficiency but causes us to turn to others in humility asking for their help. Repentance is turning to God for help, the opposite of the idolatrous practice of turning to a substance or process for help.

This repentance is the principle depicted in the story of the Prodigal Son, the touching story told by the Lord Jesus Christ to illustrate the attitude a person takes when he is truly repentant. The Prodigal Son turned around 180 degrees. The attitude of God in response to his repentance demonstrates grace instead of law.

The boy was not acting sorry to manipulate his family; he *was* sorry. This sorrow motivated him to return, to apologize and to humble himself and take his lumps just to be near his dad again. The father, unwilling to see his younger son suffer any longer, ignored the son's offer to "pay him back." The truth is that the debt was greater than the son's ability to pay. In the same way, God pushes aside the pitiful offer the repentant man makes to "pay Him back," extending instead, through grace, His love and forgiveness.

The older brother is like many Christians, sons in good standing who think they deserve the favor of God for "sticking with Him" through hard times. But the father wants the older brother to realize that he can never deserve his father's favor, it is given to him the same way it is given to the boy who needs to repent—by grace. In withholding forgiveness from his brother, the older son shuts himself out of experiencing grace, too.

All of us who are addicts need to ask God to take us back home. God certainly wants us home with Him where we belong.

The following prayer may help the addict get started on his new life back home with his heavenly Father:

"Father, I have been like the Prodigal Son. I have taken everything You have given me and used it for my selfish pleasure. I have sinned against You and know I am not worthy to be Your child. But in this story the father receives the son back anyway. Would You take me back? Would You forgive me? I give my life to Jesus Christ and ask You to cleanse me from my guilt of sin. Thank You for hearing me. In Jesus' name. Amen."

The prayer prayed from a sincere heart is the one God hears. If you are an addict and have already accepted Jesus Christ, realize that you are still like the second son. Before you ever came to Him, God knew you would have this struggle with addiction and accepted you anyway. He's waiting to see your form on the road home. The Father Himself will meet you and help you make your way back.

But now, for every addict who has come home to God, there is another step to healing, which we will discover in the next chapter.

16
Choosing
Healthy
Relationships

If we walk in the light as He Himself is in the light, we
have fellowship with one another, and the blood of Jesus
His Son cleanses us from all sin.   1 John 1:7

Arriving in Canaan sometimes depends on whom you are
walking beside. The alliances the children of Israel made
affected drastically the outcome of their journey. Joshua and
Caleb escaped the sword and the plagues of the wilderness by
keeping their eyes on God and submitting to Moses' leadership. They walked into their inheritances with style and grace,
mature in the Spirit. But behind them lay the graves of several
outstanding rebels.

Notice that none of the rebels—including Korah, Dathan,
Abiram, Nadab and Abihu—acted alone. Someone else was
always in concert with them, feeding their egos and fueling
their complaining flames. For many who didn't make it, nothing more than their choice of friends determined the outcome
of their wilderness experience.

Likewise, the addict who hopes to subdue addiction must learn to choose his relationships wisely. The problem is that many addicts do not know how to choose relationships that will enhance their lives. Many were brought up in dysfunctional homes with parents and siblings who knew nothing about selecting friends. Unfortunately, we tend to select friends who are like us, often having the same dysfunctions.

This fact of nature became clear to me while I stood at the multistory underground aquarium at Disney World. Although the aquarium was enormous and contained hundreds of varieties of fish, the members of each species always swam together.

Human beings are like that, swimming in schools with others who are similar to us. We choose our friends by the criterion of sameness. But this exclusivity gets us into trouble. Because we feel comfortable around someone does not guarantee it will be a healthy relationship. We often feel comfortable when our distorted moral values are corroborated or when our false ideas remain unchallenged. Addicts are thrown together in fellowship with other active addicts on the basis of their need for the same addictive substance or process. Their unholy alliance leads to further compulsive behavior and danger.

Pete and Sally, a young couple with three small children, have great difficulty with relationships and do not know why. As we hear their story, let's examine some of the main reasons why relationships either fail or never materialize.

Pete and Sally

Pete and Sally have been Christians for seven years and have lived in three different states as a result of Pete's job.

Pete is a recovering alcoholic. Although he has never opened himself to treatment, he abstains from liquor and attends church services in order to replace the alcohol that once ruled his life. Sally is compulsive about food, a people addict, emotionally unstable and lapsing often into depression. A talented musician and cook, Sally wants to be the homemaker portrayed in Christian women's magazines. But because of a lack of role models early in her childhood (she was the child of an alcoholic mother), the "virtuous woman role" remains a mystery to her.

In the seven years that Pete and Sally have been Christians, they have belonged to six churches. The pattern of their relationships is always the same. Upon coming to a new church, Pete and Sally pass through a period of infatuation. They view each new pastor, each new peer group and program as exciting, challenging and "the closest place to heaven on earth."

Not long into the infatuation period, however, it is usually Sally who notices first that "things are not as they should be." In their last church, the pastor did not live up to her expectations of a man of God. When he did not elevate her to a position she wanted, and when Pete and Sally could not get close enough to the pastor to become a confidante, they assumed he had an air of pride and superiority and was rejecting them as persons. Soon Pete and Sally began to notice other aspects of the church that were less than heavenly. The attitude of the church librarian seemed to be too possessive. The church spent too much money on the decor rather than on missions. And it was hard to make new friends.

They began to feel they must be in the wrong place. Everything was supposed to go smoothly in the Christian life, so why did Sally feel disillusioned? Self-pity loomed large and she lapsed into depression.

Pete and Sally's pattern is common among many addicts and ACOAs seeking out relationships in the Church. Never having been exposed to "normal" people, they tend to expect perfection, especially from authority figures. Because Sally's parents failed her early in life, she bears a deep-seated resentment toward all authority figures—a resentment to which each pastor eventually falls victim.

When her expectations of the pastor and others are not met, she sees in them the parents who failed her. Because her methods of communication are dysfunctional, she does not know how to maintain relationships without manipulation, triangling and avoidance. She does not know how to express herself appropriately. Her anger, most of which is closet anger, comes out in other ways affecting both the relationships she wants to develop and the way others view her. And soon she is affecting Pete's views. Not only are Sally and Pete incapable of commitment; they are unhealthy people who can be dangerous to other Christians.

The following is a test through which to sift any potential relationship.

Is This Relationship Healthy?

_____ 1. Is my friend a born-again Christian?

For anyone taking steps to restore a relationship with God, it is important to limit the closest friendships to those who are friends of God. "Whoever wishes to be a friend of the world makes himself an enemy of God" (James 4:4). If you don't know where a friend stands, ask him. If you have to ask, it can be a warning sign.

217

_____ 2. Does my friend follow the Lord with the same commitment I have or is there an "unequal yoke" between us?

The apostle Paul compares the relationship between Christian and non-Christian using the metaphor of two oxen yoked together plowing a field. An ox plows at a pace right for him, within his capacity. Place him with an ox of different temperament and maturity and the farmer gets nowhere. The oxen cannot move forward for pulling against each other, and the yoke actually rubs wounds in their flesh. So it is with people. Differing commitment levels to the Lord can chafe and keep either person from fulfilling the will of God for his or her life.

_____ 3. Do I feel used by this person?

The motive behind the relationship is usually determined by whether or not one or both parties feel used. Sometimes the anguish is a result of a lack of communication, but sometimes it is because the other person is selfishly expecting to exceed the boundaries of the relationship.

_____ 4. Does my friend have my spiritual well-being at heart?

If so, you will not have to compromise your spiritual life to be friends, but will be free to do what you believe the Lord wants you to do.

_____ 5. Is my friend an addict or compulsive person?

Co-dependents draw addicts like steel to a magnet often before the addiction is even apparent. You will soon be a victim of the selfish behavior of the addict who has not been in recovery for a long time. Let go and let God work.

_____ 6. Does this person know himself and have a handle on his own weaknesses?

A person who does not know himself is in denial about his weaknesses. Such a person is susceptible to your control and will become angry with you without understanding why. To be honest about yourself is one of the greatest gifts you can bring to a relationship.

_____ 7. Does this person speak the truth to me because he loves me?

Your closest friends should be able to gently tell you the truth. No relationship can grow in an atmosphere of nit-picking, but do you allow them to speak the truth to you? If they do not feel free to do this, you may be intimidating them, or they may possess an unhealthy "fear of man." There won't be much openness and honesty in these relationships.

_____ 8. Do I feel manipulated by my friend?

Does this person seem to have a hidden agenda? As a pastor's wife, I have experienced trouble in this area. From time to time some women who befriend me want to use our friendship to make their views on church issues known to the pastor. I come away from conversations with them feeling like a carrier pigeon and uncomfortable in my soul. When you feel manipulated, detach yourself emotionally, laying the relationship on the altar.

———————— 9. Does this person flatter me for the sake of gaining an advantage?

People who gush over you usually have a hidden agenda. An elderly pastor I know warned a group of young ministers, "Watch out when visitors shake your hand and say, 'This was the voice of a god and not of a man.' If you listen to 'em, you'll wind up like Herod—dead, eaten by worms!" Friendship built on flattery and deceit has a hidden dagger, as it did for the Herod in the first century who listened to the accolades of men.

————————10. Does this person really know me, or is he infatuated with an unrealistic idea of who I am?

The person who flatters you is sometimes infatuated with an unrealistic perception. He may have been wounded by another person and be looking for the "perfect" replacement, whether pastor, friend, business associate or spouse. Because these people are usually unable to survive the discovery of your faults, it is unwise to commit yourself emotionally.

————————11. Do I have to give up other healthy relationships in my life in order to be this person's friend?

An emotionally scarred individual looks for a friend who will be his or hers exclusively, probably to replace a parent's love never received. The "friend" who demands your undivided affection is looking to you for something only God can provide—security. Do not allow anyone to demand such exclusivity of you.

————————12. Do the people I admire spiritually feel this is a healthy relationship? Why or why not?

If you feel uncomfortable about submitting this friendship to the scrutiny of people whose advice you usually admire (although anyone can be mistaken), ask yourself why. Could it be that you know it is wrong, unsafe or unhealthy? An objective opinion from a mature Christian is a pearl of wisdom.

_____13. Is my friend jealous of me or others?

Jealous people have their own selfish interests at heart. They will not be happy in your accomplishments or seeing you doing God's will. Eventually their own insecurities will cause them to loathe you.

_____14. Does my friend monopolize my time?

A friend who monopolizes your time is looking to you for emotional validation, driven by insecurity and crippled in the ability to make other friends.

_____15. When I'm around him or her, do I feel spiritually edified?

What flows into your spiritual river from this friend's stream? Does he or she focus on Jesus Christ rather than on mundane problems only? If the fruit of joy is missing, ask yourself why. The best relationships do not merely provide emotional support, but enhance our desire to walk with God.

_____16. Is this friend growing spiritually or simply acting spiritual to be my friend?

If your friend has a relationship with the Lord, he will want to share with you what he has gleaned in prayer and in the Bible about God, himself and others. If he has nothing to contribute, he might be following God through you, using you as a crutch or substitute for God. You may even have become his "idol."

_____17. Does this person betray the confidences of others to gain my sympathy or approval?

The insecure individual will resort to gossip to gain your friendship. But what does he tell others about you? The Scripture says, "A perverse man spreads strife, and a slanderer separates intimate friends" (Proverbs 16:28). Gossip is toxic waste deposited in a tributary, which, in turn, will flow into you.

_____18. Do I have the right to say no and still be his or her friend?

If you are in the Mafia, the answer is no. But you should be free as a Christian to say no when the boundaries of your relationship have been broken down. If you don't feel you can say no, you will feel manipulated, obligated and resentful. If you cannot say no, you will be unable to express anger.

_____19. Can I be myself—my true self with my own feelings and opinions—and still remain his or her friend?

Your closest friends can know all about you— even what you look like without makeup—and love you just the same. You should be able to relax completely and still maintain their respect and the boundaries of the relationship. If another's expectations of you are unrealistic and you are not free to share openly, the relationship is dysfunctional. If there are unmentionable topics such as life-controlling problems, things about which the other person is in denial, you are operating already by the unwritten law of silence, a sign of dysfunction.

_____20. Does this person have a besetting sin he or she is unwilling to face?

Friends not honest with themselves will not be honest about other matters in a relationship. People who want to live in sins like slander, illicit sex, stealing, lying and manipulation will poison you. Holiness to the Lord should be a condition of any friendship.

_____21. Does this person have a rebellious, suspicious or discordant attitude toward authority figures?

The rebellious person subconsciously seeks an issue to oppose or a flaw in an authority figure. He excuses himself on the basis of his "righteous" indignation toward all authority. This person has been disappointed by an authority figure and treats everyone accordingly— possibly a symptom of his perfectionism. You will likely be the next victim, and associating with him will likely lead you to buck authority, too.

_____22. When I'm around him, do I feel the need to parent, manage or rescue him?

Unless this "friend" is your child, this should be taken as a sign of a co-dependent relationship. You may need his problem or crisis on which to thrive emotionally. If you are the parent, is the child an adult? Should he be taking responsibility for himself? Is his life out of control because he depends on you to shore him up? Find ways to ease yourself out from under this unhealthy responsibility.

_____23. Is this person's interest in me sexual?

You may think the relationship is friendly, but are your emotions stirred in this direction? Persons of the opposite sex often are in denial about the true nature of a male/female relationship. Are you committing emotional adultery—leaning on another's spouse for emotional support? Can you talk to someone of the same sex about your problem or are you dependent emotionally on this person alone? This common form of co-dependency is indicative of an unhealthy relationship. By the same token, with the rise of homosexuality in our culture, inordinate same-sex emotional ties should be severed immediately. The sexually perverse person will dominate and control those around him or her.

_____24. Do I have to compromise my moral and ethical values to remain close?

If so, you are like a city whose walls are broken down. You are vulnerable emotionally to a person leading you out of the will of God and into sin. This relationship should be discarded.

_____25. Do I trust this person? Why or why not?

If you cannot shake a gut-level feeling that your friend is untrustworthy, look for the reason. If you do not trust easily, it may be an old fear cropping up. But many times this negative feeling is the first sign of spiritual discernment. Don't be surprised when you see other symptoms of an unhealthy relationship.

Score: The following answers indicate the relationship is unhealthy:
No—1, 4, 6, 7, 12, 15, 18, 19, 25
Yes—3, 5, 8, 9, 11, 13, 14, 17, 20, 21, 22, 23, 24
Unequal—2
Infatuated—10
Acting—16
If I answered yes to 21 and 24, I would sever the relationship immediately or detach myself from the emotional highs and lows of an addict who is a relative.

If I had more than five of the other answers above, I would beware and keep this person on the periphery of my life.

Now that we have taken the test, let's talk about the different types of relationships and about setting boundaries for current and developing relationships.

The Addict's Greatest Privilege

Different relationships contribute different streams of life into a person's character, but all relationships are not the same in intensity. To see how this works, let's look at Jesus' relationships.

Jesus was here on the most important mission ever given anyone. The redemption of mankind hinged on His obedience. He could not allow any relationship to intrude upon His consecration to God. Even those closest to Jesus were not allowed to exceed certain boundaries. No one intruded on

His devotional life, for example, until He permitted it. He often drew aside to a secluded place to pray, away from ministry, away from human need, because His Father came first. Likewise, the healthy person will always put God first. In doing so, he will not expect from others what he should be expecting from God.

The closest personal relationships Jesus had were with His disciples. Within this group of dedicated men and women, Jesus had three close friends. Peter, James and John were often selected to draw aside from the others to hear things the others did not hear. Jesus did not sin, of course, in having a special relationship with these three. He even had nicknames for James and John, whose initial fanaticism amused Him. Likewise, we should not feel guilty when God knits our hearts in especially deep relationships with other Christians.

The kinship Jesus enjoyed with these men did not afford any special honor. The mother of James and John tried to insist that this relationship should have some positional reward, but Jesus quickly dispelled any jealousy by affirming that positions were not His to give.

Around these three was a circle of nine other men whom Jesus had selected to be His closest followers. Their commitment was also based on desire rather than the promise of a position. Only one of them, Judas, represented a corrupt relationship, although Jesus knew this from the beginning. It stands as a testimony to the fact that Jesus was not afraid of what a person could do to Him and that He is willing to give everyone a chance to be His friend. At the same time, Judas was never very close to Jesus.

Around this group of twelve disciples stood a close-knit fellowship of more than seventy men, and also a band of committed women who followed Jesus from place to place.

Some consider the exclusion of women from the Twelve as a reflection against women being called to leadership roles. I believe, however, that Jesus was protecting Himself from sexual temptation. He would let no temptation deter Him from His mission. Although He made no injunction against marriage for His disciples, Jesus kept Himself for the purposes of God alone. His purity stands as a model for ministry. We cannot allow Satan to use those in our inner circle, to whom we are emotionally and sexually vulnerable, to divert us from God's will.

Beyond these circles of disciples were friends like Mary, Martha and Lazarus of Bethany, with whom Jesus was very close. His emotional ties were deep enough that the death of Lazarus made Him weep. We do not see such a display at the funeral of the widow of Nain's only son, although Jesus also raised him from the dead.

Beyond these disciples and friends, Jesus cared about others—even those like the rich young ruler, who was sincere but would not answer the call to discipleship. Jesus obviously loved Nicodemus, the Pharisee, and Joseph of Arimathea, the man whose tomb He borrowed. There were also the crowds who flocked to hear Him speak and to find healing and blessings, although Jesus did not commit Himself to them beyond teaching, healing and blessing them because He knew their motives were primarily selfish.

Like any normal person, Jesus had people who opposed Him, who took offense at what He had to say. He became angry with them, voiced His opinion with emotion and called them names that exposed their evil intentions. Like every other human being, He was surrounded by the same array of relationships and accompanying responsibilities, joys and sorrows.

The recovering addict should pay particular attention to the model given us by Jesus. His life should serve to remove any false guilt from a person attempting to put his life back together, who feels condemned because he does not have the same intense feelings of "like" and even love toward every person.

In the life of Jesus, as in everyone's life, are several types of relationships. Each of these, because they are in our lives for different purposes, produce different emotions and, therefore, must be governed by different boundaries. Knowing the purpose of a relationship is a key to what boundaries it should have. When these boundaries are violated, it is natural to experience anger and resentment. Let's examine the types of relationships.

Addiction-Prone Christians and Relationships

1. Peers

Peers are a large pool of persons from whom we choose our closest friends. They are those with whom we feel bonds as a result of experience, talent, position. Whom we regard as a peer indicates something about ourselves. In the Body of Christ, peers can add spiritual enrichment and support when others—even closest relatives—are emotionally unavailable.

2. Mentors

Mentors are persons from whom we learn. A mentor, because of who he is, commands a different level of respect and honor because he contributes knowledge and understanding into our lives. These teachers, pastors, counselors, doctors and others *whom we seek for counsel* have different emotional involvement from our peers. Because they must maintain objectivity as the boundary of that relationship, it is unrealistic and usually inappropriate to expect the same sort of emotional responses and social contacts from them as we do from other relationships.

3. Professional relationships

These are the folks at work with whom we must maintain cordial, but professional, rapport. When these boundaries break down, the company, the church or the office suffers. Expecting emotional responses from professional relationships as we would from peers is unwise and unhealthy. The boss may find it difficult to give orders to a chum. Seeking them to console, counsel or even date can be detrimental for everyone involved.

4. Relatives

These are there for life, unless the boundaries break down. Violating their trust, confidence and respect can bring wounds that last a lifetime. Relatives are there to nurture and give love, affection and attention on different levels. Jesus did not permit His mother or His earthly brothers, however, to deter Him from His calling.

The relationship with a spouse is the most intimate human relationship and the most sacred. As a result, it should provide the greatest form of emotional validation and love. No one but God can replace this type of relationship.

Someone whose emotional needs are not met by a spouse

229

and other relatives will usually look for fulfillment in other types of relationships. People from dysfunctional homes have trouble with relationships because they are usually seeking this type of affection and attention in inappropriate places and from unhealthy people.

5. *Enemies*

As with other relationships, enemies are allowed to come into our lives to test us. Sometimes their perspectives should be acknowledged because they bear a kernel of truth that a friend might not relay. How we react to enemies determines how we progress spiritually. Jesus loved His enemies, but showed them His righteous anger. He exhorted us to love our enemies and do good to those who hate us. Enemies should have boundaries and not be allowed to trample us emotionally. Remember, the people addict who is usually a "martyr," letting his enemies trample on him with no redemptive purpose in view, needs as his motto "Jesus is the Savior; I am not the savior."

Setting Boundaries

The addictive personality that fails to set boundaries for relationships becomes filled quickly with hidden anger and resentment. Or if dysfunctional friends do not know the proper boundaries, the resulting lack of communication brings a breach in the relationship. "Like a city that is broken into and without walls is a man who has no control over his spirit" (Proverbs 25:28). When the boundaries of relationships are violated, he feels violated, used and trodden down. He is angry because he has lost control over the direction of his own life. Observing the boundaries set by others and learning to set his own with God's help are important parts of becoming an emotionally healthy person.

The person who allows his boundaries to be violated constantly usually has the fear of man. The writer of Proverbs observed, "The fear of man brings a snare." The ability to be manipulated is a principal characteristic of this all-too-common fear. The one who fears others is actually afraid of the reactions of other people to the boundaries he sets for his own life. He fears saying no to others' expectations and fears what will happen if he insists on his own way—even if it is God's will. The fear of man keeps him from placing God first and, like all other fears, must be faced if he is to be victorious over it.

If the recovering addict has trouble setting boundaries, here are a few suggestions. He could approach the person who is violating a boundary and tell him gently no. He may be saying no to a request or an expectation. Fear may try to keep him from standing his ground, but he must maintain it anyway, and try to understand why he is afraid. If the boundaries continue to be violated he may have to become bolder. If a problem continues, the offender is doubtless a manipulative, intimidating person who will respond only to an ultimatum. It is not necessary to threaten, only to stand his ground. It may be necessary to move such a person to the periphery of his life, detach himself emotionally or break the relationship totally.

A people addict may have several "boundary breakers" in his life who overstep constantly. These are unhealthy people and the recovering addict should never feel wrong about moving them to the periphery. He may be the only one with enough courage, by his resistance, to help them face their own problems. It may be necessary to hang up the phone, close the front door, fire them from the company, be unavailable, or if it is his child, spank him. The intimidating person will realize he means business only when he takes action.

Fortunately, most of the people in his life will not be like this and will respect him for setting boundaries. These relationships should be given different priority levels of time and attention.

Addiction Recovery and Priority Relationships

The type of relationship will determine its priority in our lives. It is important to have clean tributaries flowing into our emotional rivers; the closest relationships, therefore, should be with those who are the healthiest. Although it is not possible to dismiss certain relationships, such as with relatives and others in the Church, emotionally unhealthy people should be kept on the periphery rather than as central friends around whom our fellowship constantly revolves.

Releasing someone may be painful. It is important for the recovering addict to let God know his feelings and tell Him that he is giving this person up to Him. He can ask Him to bring change to the individual and restore the relationship when His work in their lives is accomplished. He should not concentrate on the loss of the unhealthy relationship, but begin to focus on developing healthy ones.

The Addict's Goal: Developing Healthy Relationships

The greatest friendship described in the Old Testament was that of David and Jonathan. What Jonathan did for David was a foreshadowing of Jesus Christ, the Friend who sticks closer than a brother, the perfect model for a healthy relationship. Several aspects in the development of that friendship need to be present in any friendship that flows as a tributary into our river.

1. *A godly knitting together*

From the moment Jonathan heard David speaking to his father, Saul, Jonathan loved him and wanted to be his friend. "The soul of Jonathan was knit to the soul of David, and Jonathan loved him as himself" (1 Samuel 18:1). This foreshadows the commandment of Jesus Christ, "You shall love your neighbor as yourself" (Matthew 22:39). This love was more than emotional; it stood the test of assault and the encroachment of other human relationships. God places a love in the hearts of people who are to become close friends.

The day I met Bev, one of my closest friends, I was in Bev's sister's house when Bev walked into the living room. When we met, I felt the Lord say to me, *She will be your friend—even when others let you down.* That was seven years ago, during which time many have let me down, but not Bev. (*Warning:* God does not knit two people of the opposite sex together in this type of relationship unless they are husband and wife. Anyone who believes He does is only deluding himself and placing himself in danger of seduction.)

2. *Covenant*

When God establishes a relationship between friends and between husband and wife, there must follow a mutual commitment, a promise voiced by the mouth. The covenant between husband and wife is sealed in a marriage ceremony, but there are other types of covenants, less formal but also binding. A few common examples of covenants: when you say to a close friend, "I'll be there for you"; when you covenant to affiliate with a local church; and when you make a legal contract entering into a business partnership. A covenant protects the relationship from outside influences.

Making covenants with unhealthy people can be destructive, but committing to wholesome and Christlike relationships furthers the cause of the Gospel and the development of Christlike character. Trying to make a covenant with someone when God has not knit your hearts feels "artificial" and is jumping ahead of God.

3. *Vulnerability*

When two people commit to friendship, vulnerability between them follows. When David and Jonathan made their covenant, Jonathan gave him his robe. Prince Jonathan's robe set him apart as heir to the throne. Whenever Jonathan was seen on horseback, his robe, bearing the crest of the house of Saul, spoke for him: "There is Prince Jonathan, the next king of Israel." Giving David his robe was a symbol of humbling himself, becoming David's peer in order to be his friend. The act also proved to be prophetic for, indeed, it was David who became the next king of Israel. In the same way, Jesus gave up His life that we may wear His mantle.

To seal the covenant of friendship between them further, Jonathan gave David his armor, his sword, his bow and his belt. This represented a commitment of love, a letting down of guard. Regardless of circumstances, Jonathan was saying he would never take up the sword against David.

Even as Jesus laid aside His garments to wash the disciples' feet, and His equality with God to become a servant unto death, we should drop all masks, facades and hidden agendas and enter relationships with honesty and forthrightness. We must allow ourselves to become vulnerable and open to a friendship, whatever it brings. If it is a healthy friendship, the result will enhance our relationship to Jesus Christ.

4. Fellowship

David and Jonathan built pon this covenant a fellowship that survived until Jonathan's death. Even though Jonathan felt compelled to be loyal to his father, his friendship to David stayed true. Friendships have difficulty surviving without fellowship and communication. If we walk in the light of a Christlike life, those who want to follow Christ will also desire our friendship, and we will find ourselves walking in close relationships with many of them.

Until the emotions have been healed, a relationship like that between David and Jonathan is impossible. But once healing takes place, the relationships we once thought were impossible become possible through God.

Now that we have talked about developing healthy personal relationships, let's go on to the next step in addiction recovery, learning how to maintain and prevent relapse. Do you know the warning signs? Get ready for another quiz!

17
Conquering
Relapse

The voice of Moses was heard above the multitude of settlers—once slaves but now a vast army ready to go into the
Promised Land. All but a few had lost their parents to the
bitter wilderness journey. But their struggle had not been in
vain. Under Joshua's leadership, Israel would fulfill its destiny
as the people of God.

But as the crowd stilled to hear the last words of the
prophet, Moses' tone was somber. "All the commandments
that I am commanding you today you shall be careful to do,
that you may live and multiply, and go in and possess the
land which the Lord swore to give to your forefathers. And
you shall remember all the way which the Lord your God
has led you in the wilderness these forty years, that He
might humble you, testing you, to know what was in your
heart, whether you would keep His commandments or not"
(Deuteronomy 8:1–2).

The taking of the land would not be easy. There would be

battles, struggles they had never known before, the ruthless subduing of their enemies, the backbreaking labor of planting, plowing and reaping. And there would be a new temptation, to forget the lesson their forebears had learned from the pain of slavery, the sun-bleached desert, the bewilderment of being lost, wandering in a strange place with no one to turn to but God. The temptation to forget would be their downfall unless they remembered.

Sober is not a word to be used only by alcoholics and drug addicts. Every addiction is all-consuming. It touches every part of a person—his body, his mind and his spirit—corrupting him into a hollow shell of what he could have been. Whether it is chemical addiction or process addiction, its power can never be minimized. Staying sober is more than abstinence. The battle to "take the land" involves a continual struggle with the graveclothes of addictive behavior—the argumentativeness, the bitterness, the compulsivity, the self-centeredness, the blindness to its effects, denial of its presence, and, strongest of all, the apathy.

Becoming apathetic about addiction's subtle traps holds within its power the ability to return the addict to bondage. Just as "a sow, after washing, returns to wallowing in the mire" (2 Peter 2:22), the addict will fall into relapse unless he maintains a healthy respect for his ever-present enemy. Linda learned this lesson the hard way.

Linda

Linda's heartbreaking battle with addiction began in the Christian orphanage where she was brought as an eight-year-old. Her grandmother had no other choice but to leave her in the care of strangers when Linda's parents were killed in an automobile accident. Her grandmother's small pension was barely enough to pay for her tiny apartment. There was nothing extra for rearing a child.

Years of loneliness followed because Linda could never get over the feeling of having been abandoned. Her grades were never good, but she cultivated a sharp wit and had been blessed with a beautiful voice. Forced to go to church with the other kids from the orphanage, Linda sang obediently in the church choir; but when high school graduation came, she vowed to get out of the orphanage any way she could.

Out on her own, Linda began singing in nightclubs and bars where, each night after her performance, she rewarded herself with a large meal and several drinks. Her figure soon ballooned out of proportion, but her singing voice still welled up powerfully out of her soul and moved audiences to standing ovations. Soon she was performing in better and better places.

The next five years of Linda's life were spent trying to fill her aching soul with the glamour of the entertainment world. But as her popularity grew, Linda's life deteriorated. She had slept with practically every man she knew and had cultivated a life-controlling drug habit. She had become addicted, not only to food, but to speed and cocaine. The addictive tornado swirled through her life. In a depression, she stumbled through the grocery store one day pulling junk food off the shelves when she heard a familiar voice.

A woman Linda had known from the church where she had sung as a child recognized her and began to talk. She told Linda about a spontaneous, unorganized revival that had swept the church. When the woman invited Linda to come, she didn't refuse. The next night she found herself sitting in the same pew she had sat in as a child. At the end of the message, she made her way to the altar with the rest of the throng to give her life to Jesus.

Miraculously, she felt no further need for drugs and was able to flush all the pills and booze down the toilet without even a twinge of regret. She kept waiting for withdrawal to start, but it never came. When she told her pastor, he called her up to testify at the next service about what God had done.

Tearfully, she told her testimony with such emotion that the congregation laughed and cried for the next fifteen minutes. Then she was asked to sing. Her voice, welling up this time by the convicting power of the Holy Spirit, so moved the audience that they sat spellbound in their seats for several seconds after the last note. Then people began making their way to the altar. More than fifty people gave their hearts to Jesus Christ that night, and Linda couldn't have been happier. She felt a warmth, love and acceptance she had never known before and looked forward to her next opportunity to be used of God.

She didn't have to wait long. Her phone began to ring. Calls were coming in from nearby churches and groups, as well as from neighboring states, asking her to give her testimony and sing. Soon Linda was scheduled for several services and meetings every week. She had little time for her own church anymore and her personal devotions were on hold, but at each meeting she felt the sense of God's presence with her while she sang, so she felt sure nothing could be wrong.

Linda had always been compulsive, but thinking that her old ways were things of the past, she fell in love with and married a Christian man whose testimony of miraculous deliverance from drugs was much like hers. For several months her life seemed finally to be taking a turn toward normalcy. Addiction was behind her; now she could get on with living.

239

But Linda was under a new kind of pressure, the expectations of the Christian community. She no longer felt the elation over her salvation she once had. People still came to the altar, but in all the flurry of activity, she felt that Jesus had been left sitting somewhere, and she didn't know where to find Him.

Linda's pastor encouraged her to keep on with her Christian meetings, but her husband wasn't so eager. He often shook at times and couldn't give up cigarettes. His argumentativeness escalated and words flew like darts into Linda's already fragile emotions. He knew just how to hurt her, and a day seldom passed without some assault. Linda began to take a sleeping pill each night to calm her down.

The day her husband left was a day she would remember always. While she was gone to a meeting, he took the checkbook and wiped out their account. He left town, taking not only the money but Linda's self-esteem and her last hope for a normal life. Within two short years she had fallen back into depression.

She continued her meetings, but felt like a hypocrite. Gone was her excitement about God, her financial security and her hope. It was then she remembered speed. Believing she was no longer addicted, she decided that just one pill wouldn't hurt. She swallowed it down with some cooking wine. In a few minutes she was out of depression. She hadn't felt like doing anything for weeks and now, in a little over an hour, she cleaned her house, cooked dinner and made an appointment at the beauty shop. But after several hours, the depression settled in again.

Too embarrassed to seek help, Linda vowed she would never take speed again. But the next morning, just to wake up, she took another. It wasn't long until she was taking speed daily. But when the calls to sing began to wane, Linda felt abandoned by God, by Christians, by her husband, and faded back into the oblivion of addiction. Ten more years passed before—happily—she finally went for help.

Linda's story carries a cautionary message that is important for us to look at.

The Reality of Relapse

The possibility of relapse is *part* of an addiction.

Whether it is a matter of days, weeks or years, returning to the addictive cycle at least once seems inevitable. The relapse has some of the characteristics of the original addiction. Before relapse, the addict reaches a state of denial about the nature and effects of addiction. He ignores warning signals, such as more-intense-than-normal reactions to circumstances. Until the relapse occurs, he is often unaware that it is happening. Let's look at some of the symptoms of relapse.

Get a pencil and place a checkmark beside any of these symptoms you may have experienced recently.

Symptoms of Impending Relapse

_____ 1. Too much too soon

The joy of the addict's newly found freedom leads him to take on more responsibility than he is capable of handling in his weakened state. Unfortunately, Christians often place recovering addicts in positions of responsibility before they have developed enough spiritual muscle power to handle them. The truth is that many addicts may never be able to handle the same amount of responsibility as others without heading toward relapse. How different Linda's story might have been had she had time to recover.

_____ 2. Exhaustion

In an attempt to control his craving, the physically and emotionally drained addict frequently turns to cross-addictions such as food, sweets and work to relieve his anxiety. By doing so, he places himself at risk of relapse.

In the wilderness, the nation of Israel was attacked from the rear by the Amalekites. Their prey were the stragglers, those who were tired and weary and fainting along the way. In the same way, we are vulnerable to spiritual attack when we are not at our best physically and emotionally. Our weaknesses devour our spiritual progress. Staying addiction-free requires learning our limits—a hard lesson for a perfectionist or overachiever.

_____ 3. The myth of the instant cure

Linda did not backslide from her deliverance; she was never fully healed in the first place. Linda was a binge addict, able to stop in an emotionally charged moment, but the damage done by chemical abuse left wounds in her emotions and her mind. Her habits and behavior continued to be compulsive-addictive in nature. Every addict who is able to abstain needs some form of treatment in which the habit patterns and behavior surrounding addiction are broken. Even after treatment, he should re-

member that he is in the *process* of being
healed, cured and delivered.

_____ 4. Negative emotional states

Regardless of the length of time since the
addict's last use, negative emotional states and
painful memories can produce enough stress to
cause him to go back into the addictive cycle.
For this reason, guarding his emotional health
and making himself aware of how he is feeling
are essential to maintaining freedom.

_____ 5. Relationship problems

Recovering addicts are usually warned by
support groups against trying to develop roman-
tic relationships while in treatment and initial
recovery. The highs and lows of love can become triggers for relapse into addiction. The
person he or she attracts is usually a co-
dependent. As a result, the relationship more
than likely is an unhealthy one. Too often
when the breakup occurs, it's back to addiction.

_____ 6. Apathy

The compulsive-addictive person throws
himself into the recovery process as compulsively as he does everything else in life. But
when the topic of addiction begins to be less
exciting, he drops his guard. Soon old addictive
behaviors creep in, and he is vulnerable to relapse.

Becoming apathetic to the addiction, no
longer viewing it as life-threatening, is dangerous and a set-up to the addictive cycle. Apathy

is usually followed by thoughts like "Addiction is no longer a problem for me," "I've been sober for years; there's no way I'll go back to it," "It's time to move on to something else and forget all this addiction business, anyway." Believing this will lead to relapse or cross-addiction before he knows it.

———— 7. Major life changes

Serious illnesses, moving from one location to another, losing a loved one, getting married, having children, losing a job or starting a new one and dozens of other major crises common to man can all be used to trigger addiction. Impulsive decision-making during these times of crisis can bring despair, triggering relapse. During such times, the recovering addict should step up attendance at support groups and share his feelings with the group openly. It may be advisable to seek counseling and certainly the prayer support of his church—not only for the crisis, but for the addiction.

———— 8. *Positive* emotional states

One alcoholic confessed to me that it was not depression that drove him to drink, but the feeling of elation over success and the subsequent lifting of stress, the desire to celebrate. Positive emotional states can lead to carelessness. When emotions polarize quickly from low to high, the shock can trigger the addictive cycle. It is necessary for the recovering addict to guard himself during the "good" times as well as the bad.

_____ 9. Self-pity

Self-pity is a negative emotional state, and almost always triggers relapse. The addict has sown a lot of heartache. When he begins to reap the results, the temptation to feel sorry for himself can be overwhelming. Self-pity is the first domino to fall in the emotional chain. Learning to recognize self-pity when it seeps in to fragile emotions and to readjust thinking are two keys to stopping the addictive cycle before it begins to spin.

_____10. Forgetting to be grateful

Recovery groups encourage the addict to maintain an attitude of gratitude for what God is doing. Had the children of Israel continued to be thankful and grateful for God's interventions and provisions, there would have been no breeding ground for self-pity.

_____11. Expecting too much from others

Elated over his newly discovered freedom, the addict becomes impatient with others who cannot yet trust him. The fact escapes him that he has promised others many times before that he will change, only to relapse. When others do not show the same excitement over his recovery, the addict interprets this as a sign of rejection, which can lead to relapse.

But not only does the addict expect instant acceptance from others before he has regained their trust, he is often impatient with others who are struggling with the same addiction. He can become self-righteous and proud unless he is made aware of his attitude. For this reason, the addict must maintain humility in the face of his addiction. He is one pill, fix, drink or binge away from becoming re-addicted. It walks beside him—not a mile behind him. He must choose each day to walk in freedom.

_____12. Letting up on discipline

Neglecting prayer and Bible reading cuts us off from the source of our strength, which is God alone. Self-sufficiency creeps back into the life of the addict who neglects these disciplines.

_____13. Failure to handle cravings and urges

Addicts can sometimes go for years without experiencing a craving, but cravings can reappear at any time. An action so benign as driving past a bar or seeing a TV commercial can trigger the craving. The wise addict anticipates the craving and decides that he will use a key defense. He will *distract himself until it subsides*. The longer the length of time between the craving and the last use, the shorter the period of craving. Knowing what is happening makes it easier to resist. It cannot be overemphasized to the substance addict that his cravings are not the result of defective moral character or spiritual deficiency, but rather are a biological response. If craving persists he should call a friend to talk, distract himself with a harmless activity, pray—or all of the above. If he doesn't give in, this, too, shall pass.

Score: Checking more than four of these symptoms indicates you would benefit from counsel and the help of a support group. You may be well on your way to relapsing into your addiction, but it isn't too late if you act now.

What steps can we take to keep from relapsing into addiction? In the next chapter, we will look again at Linda and see what advice she followed that brought her back from addiction's cruel grasp.

18
Possessing the Land

For this is the will of God . . . that each of you know how to possess his own vessel in sanctification and honor, not in lustful passion, like the Gentiles who do not know God . . . for God has not called us for the purpose of impurity, but in sanctification. 1 Thessalonians 4:3–5, 7

We come now to the end of the pilgrimage and the stage addicts look forward to: possessing the land.

Possessing the land was the dream of the Hebrews when they left Egypt. The first generation failed to do so, becoming aimless wanderers, moving from camp to camp with no hope of ever seeing their dream come to pass. Their unwillingness to let God teach them how to take control of their inheritance caused them to lose their purpose for living. They all were defeated because they had given up on God. That is, all except two old men.

The day the twelve spies came out, they had a discouraging report, but two were not ready to quit. Joshua and Caleb tried to encourage the Hebrews to trust God and were told that they alone would live to see Israel take the land. It isn't hard to imagine Caleb, sitting each night around his fire, sharpening his arrows, telling his children about all he had seen and communicating to them a vision of the wonderful life that lay in store for them. While others murmured and complained, Caleb spent his time reviewing every inch. Like his ancestor Abraham, who was told by God to look as far as he could see and walk about the amount of land he wanted to possess, Caleb mentally "saw" and "walked over" every inch.

One particular piece of property had caught his eye—the hill country. The others could have the fertile, easily taken plains. Caleb longed instead to build his house on the mountaintop on a place where he could spend his last years looking out over the land he had so long seen in his dreams.

And he got his dream land. On the day they walked over the Jordan, Caleb reminded Joshua of the day God promised it to them, and he specifically asked for the portion that he wanted so badly.

Caleb knew that this particular portion would be the hardest won because the hill country was inhabited by the giants, the very ones that frightened the first generation away. Joshua gave him permission to try to obtain the land and Caleb took his men and drove out the giants. In fact, Caleb alone of all the men of Israel was faithful to drive out his enemies and fully possess the land. He did so because, as God observed about him, he had a "different spirit" (Numbers 14:24).

In the same way, the Christian who is addicted to any substances or processes needs "a different spirit" to cause him to drive out *all* his enemies. To him, addictions and compulsions are like "giants in the land." How does he drive out the giants? Where does he go for help when his willpower is not enough?

Let's see what Linda, whom we met in the last chapter, did to rise up and take her "land."

Linda's Success Story

Linda hadn't been to church in years. One day in boredom she flopped down in front of the TV. Snapping through the cable channels, she ran across a talk show on the subject of addiction. As she listened, she recognized herself. When she heard the symptoms of addiction and the way it had affected the moral and spiritual lives of others, she knew she needed treatment. But she knew nothing about where to look for counsel and advice. She didn't want to go back to church because the memories were too painful.

Through a friend, she found a Christian addiction counselor who began to guide her on the rough road to recovery. Linda's low self-esteem, her painful past and fear of abandonment were giants that never had been killed. As a result, she hadn't been successful in "forgetting what was behind" and pressing toward the mark of Jesus Christ. Little by little, Linda and her counselor, with God's help, began to drive away the giants. After six months of counseling, she began to notice the return of joy, something she hadn't felt in years.

Along with private counseling, Linda sought out a support group. She was reluctant at first, but once she found a Narcotics Anonymous group she understood why her counselor felt it was so important. She sat through the first several meetings without saying anything. Being a Christian, she didn't agree with some things people said and how they expressed themselves, and it was hard to admit she needed to be in a peer group with a bunch of addicts, but she stayed—and she's glad she did.

The support group was built around the Twelve Steps of Alcoholics Anonymous (see Appendix II). As each recovering addict began to share feelings and experiences, Linda stopped feeling isolated and lonely in her addiction. On her fifth visit, she started talking and was surprised to discover the freedom to share. At church when she had tried to bring up her feelings, she had been at times condemned for not having enough faith. If more mature Christians couldn't accept her, problems and all, she felt God wouldn't accept her. Now if she felt the need to pop pills, it was O.K. to call one of the members of Narcotics Anonymous. They understood. They'd been there—and some were still there.

For a long time, Linda went to counseling and to group meetings, but she was still silent about God. One day her counselor said, "You are mad at God, aren't you?" Stunned by the question, Linda gulped. But instead of shoving her emotions down, this time she let them out.

"You'd better believe I'm mad at God! And all those so-called Christians, too!" Linda was shocked at the stored anger, but out of her mouth flooded years of anger at God for letting her parents die in a wreck, for making her grandmother poor, for condemning her to that awful orphanage, for her disappointment over her marriage and for the church people who ignored her problems and used her.

Linda's counselor was neither shocked nor condemning, and as Linda looked up at her through her tears, she realized the counselor had shed a few, too. For a long time, they sat in silence. Linda felt clean, as if the root of her infection had been removed. It was funny, but she didn't feel mad anymore.

It took two months more before Linda had the courage to go back to church. She started attending a small church not far from her home. It wasn't as easy to hide in the smaller church, and she found out what it meant to be accountable. She was a little surprised when the pastor didn't ask her to sing, but treated her like everyone else. Soon she was attending every service and enjoying being a regular person.

With the patient encouragement of her Christian counselor and her dogged persistence at her support group, she slowly made her way back to God and made amends with the home church family she had abandoned in her addiction.

Not every story ends this happily. It starts by recognizing the magnitude of the problem and taking the responsibility for finding help. Here are a few suggestions for finding a counselor, a treatment center, a support group and a local church.

Perhaps you have seen yourself thus far in the process of understanding addictive behavior and working toward inner wholeness. If you have, then it is equally important to your success to get help from others. I would like to speak directly to you in the rest of this book and encourage you to take the final steps toward recovery from addictive behavior.

Finding Help

In order to "possess the land," you must know what that "land" is.

The land is you. When Paul wrote, "Let each of you know how to possess his own vessel in sanctification and honor," he was speaking of the whole person. In order to fulfill God's plan for your life, you must conquer the "land" in you. Even as Adam and Eve could not control themselves and lost the Garden, so the one who cannot control himself loses his own plot of ground. But as you acquire a "different spirit," the

Spirit who patiently conquers and does not give up, you, like Caleb, can possess the land.

Possessing the land, like any other battle, requires a strategy. Having a strategy restores control to you and helps ensure victory.

Dr. Sue Barrick Miller, a psychologist and a Christian, explains it this way: "The recovering addict is scaling a mountainside. Slipping is inevitable, but strategies for handling relapse are like the branches sticking out of the mountainside—things to hold onto to keep you from sliding too far." In order to keep from sliding too far, you need to have a strategy for your body, your soul and your spirit. You need to know where to get help for each of these. The more knowledgeable, trained people who are on your side in the battle, the better your chances are for victory.

Taking care of your physical body is important to the success of your recovery. The *doctor* you choose to help your physical recovery should be knowledgeable about your particular addiction. If it is food addiction you are battling, consult a physician before you go on a diet. If you are an alcoholic or a drug addict, you need medical assistance in detoxification and monitoring of withdrawal symptoms. Depending on the advancement of the addiction, withdrawal symptoms can be fatal. Accountability to a doctor can help keep you from further damaging the body God has given you and promote good health habits that last a lifetime.

The *counselor* you choose makes an enormous difference. In choosing a counselor, feel free to ask questions about his or her own beliefs, attitudes, knowledge, and experience with addiction counseling. Counselors who are not knowledgeable about addiction counseling are not equipped with the tools to help you overcome addiction, even if they are Christians or have Ph.D.s. You need someone who can recognize symptoms of addictive behavior, recognize symptoms of denial and can confront you about the issues relating to your addiction. A counselor who has a definite agenda for treatment rather than one who approaches treatment in a disjointed, unending search offers the best care. Treatment by certified psychologists, psychiatrists and addiction counselors is often covered by insurance.

Christians generally want counselors who are Christians. If none is available, seek help from an experienced addiction counselor with high moral values who will respect and not ridicule or undermine your principles and beliefs. The counselor should be one who does not want to make you dependent on himself and whose own problems do not influence his counsel and advice.

Do not automatically discard a counselor because he does not have the same religious beliefs you have; sometimes addicts use this as an excuse to avoid issues they don't want to face. It is odd, but I have seen addicts who feel no compunction about sitting on the bar stool or frequenting the lottery ticket window for a chance at wealth suddenly feel guilty about going to a counselor, support group or treatment center that is not "totally Christian." Remember that the counselor is there to help you with your addiction and the emotional issues dealing with it—not to substitute for your pastor and your local church, whose focus is the spiritual aspect of recovery. In the case of knowledge about addiction and its treatment, sometimes "the children of this world are in their generation wiser than the children of light" (Luke 16:8, KJV). These people have been trained to observe the effects of addiction on the human being, God's creation. Whether a person is a Christian or not, the effects of addiction are the same. Counseling can help you understand its effects and set up a strategy to deal with them.

The addict's blindness about his own addiction extends to every area of his life. He stumbles through life groping for his way. One day the path of Jesus and His disciples crossed that of a man blind from birth. When the disciples inquired whose sin had caused him to be born that way, Jesus said, "Neither . . . but it was in order that the works of God might be displayed in him" (John 9:3). With that reply, Jesus bent down and gathered a handful of dust off the ground. He spat on the dust and made clay, and then smeared it on the man's eyes. Jesus ordered the man to go wash in the pool of Siloam. The man went to the pool Jesus had specified, washed off the mud and came away seeing.

The reason Jesus didn't simply lay His hand on him or speak the miracle into existence was to illustrate a point. If Jesus can spit on dust and use it to make a man see, He can impart something of Himself to any human being created from the dust of the ground—doctor, psychologist, addiction counselor or pastor—and use him to heal our blindness.

But there is something you must do. You must go and wash yourself in the place Jesus commands you to go. If you obey the Lord, your healing will be forthcoming. Jesus will send you to the places where He wants you to go to recover from addiction, and we should not despise any channel God so chooses to use.

If you, your family, your pastor or your counselor should recommend a stay in a *treatment center*, do not be afraid to go. You should not be embarrassed at having to go; it is more "shameful" not to care enough about yourself to get help. The addiction treatment center is not a psychiatric ward. It is a clinic with educational programs and provides group counseling and individual counseling for family and individual problems related to addiction. The average stay in a treatment center is 28 days, and many companies are happy to support their employees in their fight against addiction by giving them time off for treatment. Many insurance policies also cover addiction treatment, but some do not. You will need to check out your own coverage.

In the treatment center you will be living, dormitory style, with other addicts who are ready to attack their problems. The treatment center provides movies, lectures and group sessions to inform the addict and his family about the nature of addiction and issues related to recovery. Trained addiction counselors, physicians and psychologists usually staff the center to offer you the best intensive program for that extra push toward recovery.

While in treatment you will have opportunities to assess your condition and reflect on issues you may never have faced before. It is a humbling experience to be thrown together with other addicts from all different walks of life who have a common problem. Former First Lady Betty Ford, in her book *A Glad Awakening*, described how incensed she was to discover she would be sharing a room with four other women. But by being confronted by other addicts, she began to face her problems. It had been too easy to hide her addiction behind her wealth and position. She has since founded the Betty Ford Center, a treatment center for the chemically dependent on the grounds of the Eisenhower Medical Center in Palm Springs, California. Since its opening, it has launched thousands of addicts on the road to recovery.

In seeking a treatment center, find out all you can about it and about the staff. Many treatment centers offer Christian worship services and respect religious beliefs. Inquire about its methods of treatment and philosophy from the staff and from others who have had experience with it. Do not automatically discount a center because an addict who has been there for treatment relapses. Relapse is part of recovery, and nothing should be blamed but the addict's failure to recognize he is in jeopardy. A treatment center may be the key to opening your door to recovery.

Many counselors and treatment centers have or recommend *support groups* to supplement their treatment programs. Addicts who cannot go to a treatment center can avail themselves of the opportunity to attend a vast array of support groups for practically every form of addiction. The most effective support groups are those who practice the Twelve-Step Program.

Originating out of the Oxford Movement of Christianity, the Twelve Steps were adopted by Bill Wilson, one of the founders of Alcoholics Anonymous, and adapted to address alcoholism specifically. Today the Twelve Steps have proven effective in bringing all sorts of addicts onto the road to recovery. Millions of addicts have achieved and maintained sobriety by practicing these steps.

I believe the reason for the effectiveness of the Twelve Steps is that in their original form they were Christian in doctrine. Although some groups have generalized them to include people of all religious beliefs, the Twelve Steps remain Christian in principle. They involve admitting powerlessness over your addiction; turning to God and recognizing His superior power to rescue you; taking a fearless moral inventory; identifying and admitting wrongs to yourself and others; making restitution to those you have wronged; continuing to take moral inventory and admitting wrong promptly; and practicing these principles in all your affairs. (See Appendix II.) The person who practices these principles will undoubtedly improve the quality of his life whether or not he ever comes to Jesus for salvation. The Christian addict who practices these steps is an asset rather than a hindrance to the local church. His honesty and "up-front" way of handling human relationships make it difficult for him to harbor sin and closet anger, and he usually becomes a refreshing breath in the congregation.

Not only do the addict's wounded body and soul need treatment, but also his spirit. While the counselor, the treatment center and support group may occasionally touch on spiritual issues, the recovering addict desperately needs the love and support of a healthy *local church*. None of the other channels of treatment was ever meant to, nor does it claim to, replace the church. The ideal church is one that already has support groups for its recovering addicts. It is a sign that the Church has come out of denial about the need for addiction recovery among Christians and is supportive of the addict in his journey toward freedom.

Many churches, however, have not yet become aware of this need. If you are unable to find a church with a support group, continue active involvement in a secular support group, but locate a church where you can practice accountability. Smaller churches are good for addicts because it is much harder to slip in and out unnoticed. Large congregations in which the addict can hide his addiction or his relapse are not the healthiest atmospheres. Denial will be enforced because church attendance gives him the feeling of being religious while his whereabouts or his binges are never challenged. Large congregations often have smaller prayer groups or home Bible studies, however, to which the recovering addict can commit himself.

It is good to make your struggle with addiction known to

your pastor and become accountable to him or another leader on a weekly basis so that they may pray for you, counsel you and keep a watchful eye out for signs of relapse. The pastor who is acquainted with addiction recovery is ideal, but rare at this time. Try to find one who is sympathetic to addiction treatment, and who will confront and discipline you if necessary. *Remember, it is the addict's responsibility to initiate and maintain accountability*. It is not the responsibility of others to chase you down and know when you are relapsing.

Our church's involvement in addiction recovery came as a result of five years of prayer by a woman, a recovering addict, in our congregation. Until we understood the nature of addiction and the gradual process of the renewing of the mind necessary to subdue addiction, this woman stayed faithful to the church, attended secular support groups and prayed for us to have wisdom and understanding.

Two years ago, while reading *The Compulsive Woman* by Sandra Simpson LeSourd, my spirit was troubled by a verse out of the book of Jeremiah, "They heal the brokenness . . . of my people superficially, saying, 'Peace, peace,' but there is no peace" (Jeremiah 8:11). As my husband, Bill, and I read Sandy's story of what it took to bring her into recovery from alcoholism, we felt uncomfortable knowing that our dogmatic, traditional Christian approach had failed to help recognize the problem and bring answers to many Christian addicts who were struggling to stay free. Bill and I began to read. As our eyes have been opened, we have been able to unlock the barrier to recovery for the addicts who are willing to receive help in our congregation. Bill and I have taught on subjects directly relating to addiction recovery and have begun support groups for both recovering addicts and ACOA's based on the Twelve Steps modified for Christians. (See Appendix II.)

The woman who prayed for us has seen a miraculous answer to her prayers.

Restoring Personal Devotions

An active prayer life with a focus on reading and meditating on the Scriptures must be restored if you are to come to full spiritual health. Once the barriers of guilt have been removed, you can begin to realize that God is not mad at you for being an addict. He wants to lift you out of the quagmire of addiction. Prayer means holding out your hand to your Father and saying, "Daddy, show me how." God is only waiting for you to pray this prayer. Adopt the practice of talking naturally to God about everything. Forget the vibrating, dramatic voice and speak to Him as you would another person. Confess your fears, anger, bitterness and faults to Him and ask Him to meet your needs. Then watch how the answer comes. It may come in the form of another human being or through enlightenment on the Scriptures that brings a sense of peace to your soul or in the resolution of circumstances— but remember to thank Him.

Begin to read the Bible devotionally as though it were a love letter from God to you. Receive the correction it has to give, *but balance it out by drinking in large doses of Gospel grace.* You may want to begin with devotional literature, but don't substitute this for reading the Bible for yourself. Trying to read the Bible from beginning to end is difficult, and I'm not sure God ever intended it to be read that way, but you may want to organize your approach initially to develop a good habit. Ask the Holy Spirit to help you bite off what you can chew today and leave the rest for another day. Read about Jesus and about other characters in the Bible, as well as from the Psalms and Proverbs. Addicts have usually become spiritually emaciated for lack of "daily bread," and giving up on it usually brings relapse.

Maintaining Your Inheritance

For the recovering addict, taking the land involves recovering control over his mind, will, emotions and physical body so that his spirit, now alive with the Holy Spirit's power, is able to guide him. As he is able gradually to possess his own property, he must then learn to maintain it.

Maintaining your land is as important as obtaining it. Becoming a good steward of what God has given you means learning to protect your physical, emotional and spiritual health. No sooner will you seem to get control than you will feel assaulted by Satan's desperate attempt to regain control. His primary method of attack is temptation.

Knowing how to "possess your own vessel" (see 1 Thessalonians 4:4) means knowing your own limitations. The alcoholic will never be able to drink and should avoid places where alcohol is served; the sex addict must guard himself against exposure to sexual temptation; the soap opera addict will have to avoid daytime TV; and the compulsive shopaholic will have to cut up his credit cards. Whatever your temptation has been, you will have to be the one to realize what activities subject you to temptation and avoid them. Your conscience and your common sense will guide you if you listen to them.

What If I Slip?

What you do when you slip is the same thing you do when you stumble on a wet street corner. You recover. If you become so injured by your fall that you can't get back up alone, dial your support group.

When I began my battle with food addiction and cholesterol, my family doctor advised me well. "If you eat a piece of cake or blow it otherwise, don't accuse yourself of going off your diet. Start right back counting calories and cholesterol. Budget the relapse into your eating plan." What a relief to know that I could walk one day at a time, one meal at a time and that I could regain my step immediately if I slipped.

Getting depressed as a result of your slip will only endanger you further. Tell someone to whom you are accountable what you have done, step up support group meetings and get more treatment if necessary. *Addiction recovery, like the renewing of the mind, is a lifelong pursuit.* This incident can be used to teach you a valuable lesson: Sometimes it's good to fail and get it over with. Then you can proceed to a lifetime of freedom from worry about what you'll do if you fail! Your reaction to relapse is more important than the fact that you did. Get up and get going with fulfilling God's will for your life.

Fulfilling God's Plan for You

After you have driven the giants out and are maintaining the land God gave you to care for, it's time to turn your eyes toward God's vision for your life. What dreams do you have? What is your reason for living? What noble desires do you have? Has God called you to a specific task? If you have any godly desires or dreams, learning to maintain addiction recovery is the first step in fulfilling that plan. Possessing your own vessel enables you to take that portion of the land out there that God has reserved for you alone.

Begin to take small steps toward your larger goal. Learn to

set short-term goals for long-term projects rather than perfectionistic, unattainable ones. Do you need to go get your degree, take a correspondence course, get involved in volunteer work or help out at the church? Chances are that God has some creative idea to bring His love to others that has yet to occur to any other human being, and maybe that idea will come to you. Before you is a promised land of opportunity where you are free from the bonds of addiction to plow, to plant, to harvest and to build. Doing God's work with His help will be "no sweat" in comparison with the slavery of Egypt.

The other old Israelite who inherited the land with Caleb and the younger generation was Joshua, the new leader of Israel after Moses died. When the Hebrews walked over Jordan to take possession of their land, Joshua challenged them with the words you need to hear, "Choose you this day whom ye will serve . . . but as for me and my house, we will serve the Lord" (Joshua 24:15, KJV). Freedom from the slavery of addiction restores your right to choose and to serve. What is your choice?

Appendix I: How to Start a Christian Support Group

Addiction recovery belongs in the Church. It is a vital part of unwrapping the graveclothes of your old life and learning to walk addiction-free in Christ. Today many local churches are recognizing the need to have a special meeting for addicts and adults from dysfunctional homes in which they may open up about their addictions and receive support from others.

What does it take to have a healthy support group that fosters healing? Is healing really generated in a support group or is it just another case of "the blind leading the blind"?

In response to the need in our own church, we have begun what has become a successful support group to minister to the emotional needs of addicts and ACOAs. What we have learned may help you establish a group that is solid, stable and healthy. With this in view, I would like to suggest the following things:

1. *Talking to the pastor*

In a local church, the most successful activities either originate with or have the approval of the pastor. Since he is called by God to lead the fellowship and oversee the spiritual needs of the members, it is his right to determine what goes on in the local church. This is for your protection. If it is God's will to start a support group, he will approve it either immediately or eventually. Make an appointment with him to talk about it. Be friendly and not intimidating. Offer him material to read and have a well-defined plan to present him, being open to his modifications.

Sometimes pastors have had bad experiences with small groups becoming exclusive islands in the congregation, so be patient and prayerful. As I mentioned, someone prayed patiently for Bill and me for several years before we had the "vision" for addiction recovery in the church we pastor.

2. *Education*

Before we began our support group, we conducted a counseling course about addiction recovery in our church's adult Bible training school. This course lasted several weeks and included scriptural teaching about addiction recovery and lectures by Christian counselors and psychologists who were certified in addiction counseling.

We also conducted a teaching series on addiction to the whole church. Exposing the congregation to the need for addiction recovery brought the issue out of the darkness and into the light. Without a proper foundation, any building falls. Education about how addiction recovery is a process rather than an event is essential to having a successful support group.

3. Leadership

Support groups usually do not have leaders. It is important for the addicts and co-dependents attending groups to see themselves as peers in order for them to remain humble and open about their problems. It is necessary to have certain key people known as "facilitators" who are committed to the support group ministry, who are always there, who are knowledgeable about the issues of addiction recovery and who are honest and confrontative to prevent the meetings from taking an undesirable turn. Each member of the group can take his turn acting as a facilitator.

4. Purpose

The purpose of the support group is very different from that of the prayer group, the Bible study or social events at church. The purpose is to create and maintain an atmosphere in which addicts can receive the emotional support they need to conquer their addictions. There must, therefore, be an opportunity for each member of the group to share openly without fear of condemnation or without fear of his problems being exposed to others outside the group. It is important for the support group meetings to have a focus that is usually determined by the person who acts as the facilitator at that meeting. It is the facilitator's responsibility to keep the meeting on track and pull it back into focus if the focus is lost.

We have found that a planning board of two or three meeting once every six weeks with the pastor is an effective way to set the focus for the group. Our support group holds two or three meetings each month based on the Twelve Steps for Christians in which each member has the opportunity to share about his involvement in the Steps. At one meeting each month, the pastor teaches about an addiction-related topic, keeping the support group tied into the pastor's oversight and vision for the church. At another meeting, the members view a videotape obtained from a local addiction recovery library or hear a guest speaker, a Christian counselor or psychologist knowledgeable about addiction recovery from the Christian perspective. Varying the format slightly keeps the group exposed to healthy outside influences and open to the spiritual change that comes about through teaching.

Because the group is sponsored by a church, it is often a great temptation to turn the support group into a prayer or ministry group or a Bible study.

Believe it or not, *this defeats the purpose and squelches the way the Holy Spirit wants to move* in exposing and dealing with problems. It is too easy for an addict to sneak in and out of a worship service or a prayer meeting without confronting his addictive behavior. Prayer and ministry groups are also forums where the people addict or co-dependent loves to "shine," demonstrating his spirituality and his gifts, placating and consoling "needy" people. This plays into his problem rather than shattering the denial surrounding it.

Although Bill and I pastor our church, we do not attend the support group meetings except to teach on the designated day. We have found that the presence of the pastor often inhibits group discussion. It is too easy to turn the group meeting into an "ask the pastor" forum or a counseling session.

5. *Guidelines*

In order to prevent the loss of focus, it is necessary for the Christian support group to have guidelines that govern the meeting and the group discussion. The guidelines should be read at the beginning of each meeting and referred to by the facilitator if the meeting loses its focus. The following is the list of guidelines we use for the support group sponsored by our church.

1. The discussion is directed, but not dominated, by the facilitator.
2. The person who is sharing is to receive the undivided attention of all others in the group.
3. The person sharing should feel free to share openly and honestly without being condemned, confining him or herself to the topics at hand and considering the needs of others to speak.
4. Members of the group should refrain from counseling, advice-giving and managing the lives of those sharing. (Confronting the relapsing addict, however, is essential.)
5. Members of the group should also refrain from personal ministry to individuals, such as laying on of hands, prophecy, deliverance and prayer counseling, as this support group is not a substitute for a church meeting and is not the proper context for these ministries.
6. This support group is not a substitute for pastoral counseling, psychological or psychiatric treatment, group therapy, the local church or other support groups that may be helpful to the individual's life.
7. Everything shared in the group must be kept confidential and not discussed outside the group.

If your support group contains both addicts and those who are not addicts but are there to receive support as codependents, such as ACOAs, it is important to separate the groups. The addicts must deal with their problems in an open and confrontative manner and are usually, but not always, much more vocal than co-dependents. ACOAs, for instance, are often intimidated by addicts whose personalities and behavioral characteristics are similar to the parents they feared. If addicts attend the ACOA meetings, the addicts share openly while the co-dependents watch them silently, intimidated, relating to addicts in the same way they always have. If addicts need a forum to discuss co-dependency issues, assign one meeting every month or six weeks in the addicts' support group to deal with that topic. When I sought advice from Christian addiction counselors and psychologists about starting our support group, all of them emphasized that addicts should be separated from co-dependents in the support group setting.

6. Format

Establishing a format for the meeting facilitates smooth operation and creates a stable environment. Each support group meeting is opened by the facilitator for the particular meeting who welcomes everyone, prays briefly and gives the announcements.

Each member of the group then introduces himself in the following manner: "My name is Penny and I'm an alcoholic." This helps break denial concerning the problem and places each member on equal footing, recognizing his need and humbling himself for the purpose of giving and receiving support in the group setting. Although a Christian is much more than his problem, he must learn to accept the fact that he is a new creature living in an "addictable body." Addictions may reactivate, quenching the Spirit, unless the addict remains humble before God *and* his problem.

The facilitator then leads the group in reciting "The Christian Twelve Steps." (See Appendix II.) The program for the day, which consists of either a group discussion, a video or a lecture, follows next. The time frame for the meeting needs to be firmly established—usually at an hour and a half. At the appointed time, the facilitator closes the group discussion and receives an offering to be used for the room rental (if required), the utilities and any resource materials. The offering in our support group is given to our church, which keeps account of it and dispenses it for the designated purposes.

Following the offering is the closing prayer. The members of our group hold hands and recite in unison the entire "Serenity Prayer" by Reinhold Niebuhr:

THE SERENITY PRAYER

God grant me the Serenity
to accept the things I
cannot change;

Courage to change the things
I can; and Wisdom to know the difference.

Living one day at a time;
Enjoying one moment at a time;
Accepting hardship as the pathway to peace;

Taking, as He did, this
sinful world as it is, not
as I would have it;

Trusting that He will make
all things right if I
surrender to His will;

271

That I may be reasonably
happy in this life, and
supremely happy with Him
forever in the next. Amen.

7. The Twelve Steps

The most successful addiction recovery support groups to date revolve around some modification of the Twelve Steps of Alcoholics Anonymous. As I stated earlier, these steps have been modified by many Christian support groups to return to their original Christian focus. These steps provide a focus for the recovering addict in his daily devotional life and for group discussion at the support group meetings. See Appendix II.

The support group in our church uses *The Twelve Steps—A Spiritual Journey*, which is a working guide based on biblical teachings for adult children from addictive and other dysfunctional families authored and published by Friends in Recovery, 1201 Knoxville St., San Diego, CA 92110; (610) 275–1350.

8. Supporting Prayer

The recovery of any addict is spiritual warfare involving the need for the supernatural intervention of God and the cooperation of the addict. Although the support group is not a prayer group, it can only be helped by concentrated, supporting prayer on the part of those who are to become involved and others who desire to see it flourish. Much resistance by the enemy and emotional turmoil may be alleviated by intercessory prayer. Commitment to praying for the others in the group during private devotions is vital to the success of the group and individual recovery.

9. Anonymity

Secular support groups have found great success by protecting the anonymity of their members. Although anonymity is usually impossible in a church setting where the people already know each other, in the group meetings it is a good idea to use first names and set the tone for anonymity so that when others come they can feel free to share openly without fear.

Confidentiality must be protected or the group will fall into gossip and pettiness, destroying everything the Holy Spirit is doing. It is better not to discuss anyone's problems or reveal the opinions and events shared in the context of the meeting.

10. Perseverance

Do not give up if some of the original group members do not continue to come. Some Christians find it difficult to share feelings and problems. Remember that the group is there to offer support and be available for those who are ready to receive help. Almost anything that begins—even in the Spirit—starts with a flourish and dwindles. (Remember the story of the army in Judges 6–7!) The Lord will send those who really need and appreciate the group if you stand firm and do not give up. Many Christian counselors are anxious to find a support group based on Christian principles to which they can refer their clients for added support. Alert the Christian counselors and pastors in your area of the existence of your group and its focus. As it remains active, they will become confident that it is a permanently established group and refer others to it.

We have given the support group meeting a place of honor among all the other scheduled activities of the church and announce its date and time in the church bulletin. When the pastor mentions and praises the effectiveness of the support group from the pulpit, it adds further support and credibility to the group and encourages newcomers who are affected by addiction and ACOA issues to take an active part.

One of the special fringe benefits of our support group has been a great reduction in the amount of pastoral counseling necessary in our fellowship. As the members of the Body of Christ help each other remove their graveclothes, they learn to develop healthy relationships with their peers and find emotional support, which is the true need behind many counseling appointments.

May your group open up a highway to healing for the hurting and the oppressed.

Appendix II: A Christian's Twelve Steps to Recovery from Addiction

1. We admitted we were powerless over [name the addiction]—that our lives had become unmanageable.
2. Came to believe that God alone is powerful enough to restore us to sanity.
3. Made a decision to turn our will and our lives over to the absolute Lordship of Jesus Christ.
4. Made a searching and fearless moral inventory of ourselves.
5. Admitted to God, to ourselves and to another individual the exact nature of our wrongs.
6. Were entirely ready to have God remove all these defects of character.
7. Humbly asked Him to remove our shortcomings.
8. Made a list of all persons we had harmed, and became willing to make amends to them all.

9. Made direct amends to them except where to do so would injure them or others.
10. Continued to take personal inventory and when we were wrong promptly admitted it.
11. Sought through prayer and meditation to improve our conscious contact with God, praying only for the knowledge of His will for us and the power to carry that out.
12. Having had a spiritual awakening as a result of these steps, we tried to carry this message to addicts, and to practice these principles in all our affairs.

"A Christian's Twelve Steps to Recovery from Addiction" was modified and adapted from the Twelve Steps of Alcoholics Anonymous printed below, and reprinted and adapted with permission from Alcoholics Anonymous World Services, Inc.

The Twelve Steps of Alcoholics Anonymous

1. We admitted we were powerless over alcohol—that our lives had become unmanageable.
2. Came to believe that a Power greater than ourselves could restore us to sanity.
3. Made a decision to turn our will and our lives over to the care of God *as we understood Him.*
4. Made a searching and fearless moral inventory of ourselves.
5. Admitted to God, to ourselves, and to another human being the exact nature of our wrongs.
6. Were entirely ready to have God remove all these defects of character.

7. Humbly asked Him to remove our shortcomings.
8. Made a list of all persons we had harmed, and became willing to make amends to them all.
9. Made direct amends to such people wherever possible, except when to do so would injure them or others.
10. Continued to take personal inventory and when we were wrong promptly admitted it.
11. Sought through prayer and meditation to improve our conscious contact with God *as we understood Him*, praying only for knowledge of His will for us and the power to carry that out.
12. Having had a spiritual awakening as the result of these steps, we tried to carry this message to alcoholics, and to practice these principles in all our affairs.

Appendix III:
A Daily
Personal
Inventory

If we say that we have no sin, we are deceiving ourselves, and the truth is not in us.   1 John 1:8

"Lord, I humbly ask You to show me the truth about the exact nature of my emotional responses in the last 24 hours."

1. In the last 24 hours, have I allowed myself to become physically or emotionally exhausted?____Yes____No. If so, why and how may I avoid becoming exhausted today?

2. In the last 24 hours, have I lied to myself or others, or have I rationalized or minimized my actions and in so doing caused others harm or emotional pain?____Yes ____No. If so, how have I done so and how may I rectify these wrongs?

3. In the last 24 hours, have I become impatient with others?___Yes___No. If so, how may I change my attitude to one of forgiveness and acceptance and restore the relationship?

4. In the last 24 hours, have I become argumentative with anyone?___Yes___No. If so, how may I humble myself before him or her and restore the relationship, trusting God to change the other person if he or she needs it?

5. In the last 24 hours, have I become depressed?___Yes___No. What attitudes or circumstances led to the depression? What am I angry about?

6. In the last 24 hours, have I felt frustrated?___Yes___No. If so, how may I change my attitude and learn to accept the situation at hand, trusting God to work it out?

7. In the last 24 hours, have I felt sorry for myself?___Yes___No. If so, why and how may I change my attitude?

8. In the last 24 hours, have I acted cocky, feeling that my addiction no longer is a problem and that I have "licked it"?___Yes___No. If so, what is dangerous about this attitude and how may I change my attitude?

9. In the last 24 hours, have I become complacent in my attitude about my addiction as though it no longer poses

a threat and, therefore, diligence in discipline is no longer crucial?____Yes____No. If so, how may I restore diligence in discipline to my life?

10. In the last 24 hours, have I looked for too much from others, expecting them to have adjusted their ways as I have adjusted mine?____Yes____No. If so, describe the situation. How may I change my attitude to allow them to learn to trust me even if it takes a long time?

11. In the last 24 hours, have I let up on disciplines such as prayer, daily inventory, meditation and Bible reading? ____Yes____No. If so, how may I restore these disciplines to my life today?

12. In the last 24 hours, have I used any mood-altering chemicals including caffeine, tranquilizers, other drugs, cold medications; binged on sweets or other foods; taken any addictive substances such as alcohol or hard drugs? ____Yes____No. If I find I am unable to stop using these today, I will promptly alert my pastor, counselor or support group sponsor today.

13. In the last 24 hours, have I set goals too high to be achieved at this stage of my physical, emotional and spiritual life?____Yes____No. If so, how may I adjust these goals to be more realistic and in keeping with God's revealed will for my life today?

14. In the last 24 hours, have I been ungrateful for the blessings God has given me and pessimistic about life and others?____Yes____No. If so, I will list the blessings of the last 24 hours and thank God and others responsible for them.

15. In the last 24 hours, have I felt that "it can't happen to me" regarding addictions, attitudes or sins I see in the lives of others?____Yes____No. If so, how may I refrain from judging others and restore a humble attitude to my own heart?

16. In the last 24 hours, have I felt omnipotent, rejecting the advice and counsel of others, feeling that I already have all the answers and that others should mind their own business and stay out of mine?____Yes____No. If so, how can I submit myself to their counsel and improve my life and relationships?

"Lord, forgive me and cleanse me and give me the courage to change my actions and make amends to others I have wronged today that I may not fall into temptation."

If we confess our sins, He is faithful and righteous to forgive us our sins and to cleanse us from all unrighteousness (1 John 1:9).

Bibliography

"A Travelogue with M. Scott Peck, M.D." *Changes*, March-April 1988.

Apthorp, Stephen P. "Drug Abuse and the Church: Are the Blind Leading the Blind?" *Christian Century*, November 9, 1988.

Arterburn, Stephen. *Growing Up Addicted*. New York: Ballantine/Epiphany Books, 1988.

Backus, William. *Telling the Truth to Troubled People*. Minneapolis: Bethany House, 1985.

Barnhart, Joe E. and Winzenburg, Steven. *Jim & Tammy: Charismatic Intrigue Inside PTL*. Buffalo: Prometheus Books, 1988.

Bird, Brian. "A Wounded Soldier Comes Home." *Charisma & Christian Life*, November 1989, pp. 60–67.

Boraiko, Allen A. "Earthquake in Mexico." *National Geographic*, Vol. 169, #5, May 1986, pp. 655–675.

Carnes, Patrick J., Ph.D. *Out of the Shadows*. Minneapolis: CompCare Publishers, 1983.

Church, John. "Why Pick on Pete?" *Time*, July 10, 1989, p. 20.

Denzin, Norman K. *Treating Alcoholism: An Alcoholics Anonymous Approach*. Newbury, Cal.: Sage Publications, Sage Human Services Guides, Vol. 46, 1987.

Green, Bernard. *Getting Over Getting High*. New York: Quill Publishers, 1985.

Hirschmann, Jane R. and Munter, Carol H. *Overcoming Overeating*. Reading, Mass.: Addison-Wesley Publishing Co., Inc., 1988.

"Curing Kids Who Want It All." *Intercessors for America Newsletter*, July/August 1989, Vol. 16, No. 7/8, p. 1.

Kritsberg, Wayne. *The Adult Children of Alcoholics Syndrome: From Discovery to Recovery*. Pompano Beach, Fla.: Health Communications, 1985.

LeSourd, Sandra Simpson. *The Compulsive Woman*. Old Tappan, N.J.: Chosen Books, 1987.

Martin, Sara Hines. *Healing for Adult Children of Alcoholics: How to Break from the Past and Grow Emotionally and Spiritually*. Nashville: Broadman Press, 1988.

O'Neill, Cherry Boone. *Starving for Attention*. New York: Dell Publishing, 1982.

Ostling, Richard N. "Now It's Jimmy's Turn." *Time*, March 7, 1988, p. 47.

Phelps, Janice Keller, M.D., and Nourse, Alan E. M.D. *The Hidden Addiction and How to Get Free*. Boston: Little, Brown & Co. 1986.

Pinkham, Mary Ellen. *How to Stop the One You Love from Drinking*. New York: G. P. Putnam's Sons, 1986.

Rubin, Theodore Isaac, M.D. *The Angry Book*. New York: Collier Books, Macmillan Publishing Co., 1969.

Schaef, Anne W. & Fassel, Diane. *The Addictive Organization*. San Francisco: Harper & Row, 1988.

Seamands, Dr. David A. *Healing for Damaged Emotions*. Wheaton, Ill.: Victor Books, 1987.

Snyder, Solomon H., M.D. "Brain Function." New York: Chelsea House Publishers, *The Encyclopedia of Psychoactive Drugs*.

Spickard, Anderson, M.D., and Thompson, Barbara R. *Dying for a Drink: What You Should Know About Alcoholism*. Waco, Tex.: Word Books, 1985.

Washton, Arnold & Boundy, Donna. *Willpower's Not Enough*. New York: Harper & Row, 1989.

Wegscheider-Cruse, Sharon. *Another Chance: Hope and Health for the Alcoholic Family*. Palo Alto, Cal.: Science and Behavior Books, 1981.

Suggested Reading

Anonymous. *What Everyone Needs to Know About Sexual Addiction.* Minneapolis: CompCare Publishers, 1989.

Beattie, Melody. *Co-Dependent No More: How To Stop Controlling Others and Start Caring for Yourself.* Minneapolis: Hazelden Foundation, 1987.

Berry, Carmen Renee. *When Helping You Is Hurting Me: Escaping the Messiah Trap.* San Francisco: Harper & Row, 1988.

Ford, Betty. *A Glad Awakening.* New York: Doubleday, 1987.

Forward, Susan and Buck, Craig. *Betrayal of Innocence: Incest and Its Devastation.* New York: Penguin Books, 1979.

Forward, Susan and Torres, Joan. *Men Who Hate Women & the Women Who Love Them.* New York: Bantam Books, 1986.

Friends in Recovery. *The Twelve Steps—A Spiritual Journey.* San Diego: Recovery Publications, 1988.

MacDonald, Gordon. *Ordering Your Private World.* Nashville: Oliver Nelson Publishers, 1984, 1985.

Marshall, Catherine. *Light in My Darkest Night.* Old Tappan, N.J.: Chosen Books, 1989.

Norwood, Robin. *Women Who Love Too Much.* New York: St. Martin's Press, 1985.

O'Neill, Cherry Boone. *Starving for Attention*. New York: Dell Publishing, 1982.

Reamer, Judy with Arthur, Donna. *Feelings Women Rarely Share*. Springdale, Pa.: Whitaker House, 1987.

Seamands, David A. *Healing Grace*. Wheaton, Ill.: Victor Books, Scripture Press Publications, 1988.

Smith, Ann W. *Grandchildren of Alcoholics*. Pompano Beach, Fla.: Health Communications, 1988.

Stanley, Charles. *Forgiveness*. Nashville: Oliver Nelson Publishers, 1987.

Swindoll, Charles R. *Living Above the Level of Mediocrity*. Waco, Tex.: Word Books, 1987.

Melinda Fish is the author of five books, speaks internationally, and is a member of the pastoral team at Church of the Risen Saviour, Trafford, Pennsylvania. She and her husband, Bill, are the parents of two children.